"As a student I treasured the original Barnstone Sappho, and it is a joy to have this new version made current with the latest scholarship and enriched by four decades of further reflection. Sappho's famous voice is clear and powerful, even in the shards that remain to us, and Barnstone embraces and captures this phenomenon like no one else. This is a Sappho rendered with wisdom and heart for newcomers and connoisseurs alike."

—JEFFREY HENDERSON, Editor, Loeb Classical Library

"What amazes me is how Sappho's lyrics, composed in the seventh century B.C.E., transcend their time and place to enchant us now. In lines that are at once passionate and precise, seemingly artless and yet magical, she writes of the cycles of life and death, and of erotic desire as a sacred calling. She looks into the burning center of things, and expresses pure wonder in the evening star, the moon, birdsong. Willis Barnstone's masterful translations capture her excited praise for things of this world, making one of her prophetic observations shine with lasting truth: 'Someone, I tell you, in another time, / will remember us.' "

—GRACE SCHULMAN, author of *Days of Wonder*
and *The Paintings of Our Lives*

"If there is any final justice, which there probably isn't, the world of letters would erect a monument of Willis Barnstone and strew it with fresh wildflowers every day. I think of this Sappho collection as the finest among Barnstone's prodigious achievements."

—JIM HARRISON, author of *True North* and *Legends of the Fall*

"Sappho knew what we never tire of learning: passion makes the moment eternal. Willis Barnstone has plumbed profound layers of the ancient Greek to bring us Sappho. On his way to her, he renewed the Gnostic Gospels and the Gospels proper. Now he has sounded the deepest lyric rock of our founding and given us new sound."

—ANDREI CODRESCU, NPR commentator and author of
It Was Today: New Poems

"Willis Barnstone has brought a life dedicated to translation and a lifetime of immersion in the Greek language to give us these new and inspired translations of Sappho. With its brilliant introduction and dazzling notes, this is the book of Sappho you will want on your bedside table."

—DAVID ST. JOHN, author of
The Red Leaves of Night

"Eros has been riding Barnstone's back for years, whipping him across Spanish, French, Greek, Chinese poetry, across the poetry and prose of the biblical lands to translate from those literatures poetry, to make them new and his. Now he has embraced Sappho, with whom he has been in love for years. What he has made 'his' is a gift to us. Barnstone—lover, poet, and scholar—cannot make Sappho's fragments whole, but he makes us more aware of our loss than any other translation. He gives us the abyss, and fragments of Sappho in startling English—a few words that in ancient Greek changed its music and made the walls of the city tremble."

—STANLEY MOSS, author of *Asleep in the Garden*

SWEETBITTER LOVE

LOVE

Poems of Sappho

Translated by
WILLIS BARNSTONE

With Epilogue and Metrical Guide by
WILLIAM E. McCULLOH

SHAMBHALA
Boston & London
2006

SHAMBHALA PUBLICATIONS, INC.
Horticultural Hall
300 Massachusetts Avenue
Boston, Massachusetts 02115
www.shambhala.com

© 2006 by Willis Barnstone

Epilogue and Metrical Guide
© 2006 by William E. McCulloh

9 8 7 6 5 4 3 2 1 $2|07$

FIRST EDITION
Printed in the United States of America

Designed by Lora Zorian

⊛This edition is printed on acid-free paper that meets the
American National Standards Institute z39.48 Standard.
Distributed in the United States by Random House, Inc.,
and in Canada by Random House of Canada Ltd

LIBRARY OF CONGRESS CATALOGING-IN-PUBLICATION DATA
Sappho.
[Works. English & Greek. 2005]
Sweetbitter love: poems of Sappho / translated by Willis
Barnstone.—1st ed.
xlix, 316 p.   cm.
Includes bibliographical references.
ISBN-13 978-1-59030-175-3 (acid-free paper)
ISBN-10 1-59030-175-7
1. Sappho—Translations into English.   2. Love poetry, Greek—
Translations into English.   I. Barnstone, Willis, 1927–   II. Title.
PA4408.E5B35 2005 2006
884'.01—dc22
2005007829

for Sarah
her eyes
looking

O coronata di viole, divina
dolce ridente Saffo.

ALCEO (N. 620 B.C.E.)
SALVADORE QUASIMODO, *LIRICI GRECI*

O violet-haired, holy,
honeysmiling Psapfo

ALKAIOS (B. 620 B.C.E.)

CONTENTS

Nightingale

Walking to a Wedding

You Burn Us

Return, Gongyla

Weathercocks and Exile

Secret of My Craft

Sandal

Dream and Sleep

Age and Light

INTRODUCTION

I N Sappho we hear for the first time in the Western world the direct words of an individual woman. It cannot be said that her song has ever been surpassed. In a Greek dialect of the eastern Mediterranean, she became our first Tang dynasty poet, akin to one of those Chinese of the eighth century C.E. whose songs were overheard thought and conversation, in strict form, and who were said to "dance in chains." In her seventh-century B.C.E. Lesbos, Sappho danced in chains, singing of Kritan altars at night and fruit dreaming in a coma, and always in metrical patterns unseen but musically overheard, like her thoughts, passions, and internal dialogues.

Time with its strange appetite has modernized these ancient voices, making the Tang writer Wang Wei and the Aiolic Sappho fashionable and intimate. The East has preserved a ton of the Tang poets, or, as the Chinese would say, "ten thousand" of those golden birds in the Middle Kingdom. Despite early losses due to the fires of the book-burning emperor Qin Shi Huangdi (ruled 221–210 B.C.E.), China thereafter zealously preserved the work of its poets. But Sappho suffered from book-burning religious authorities who left us largely scraps of torn papyrus found in waterless wastes of North Africa. Such maltreatment has especially modernized her into a minimalist poet of a few but important words, connected often more by elliptic conjecture than clear syntax. But what a full living voice comes through those ruins! Every phrase seems to be an autonomous poem, including a fragment of two words describing Eros: *optais amme:* "you burn us."

One day, when the sorrows of war and hatred weary and fade, many diggers will return to the sands of infinite Egypt, to those rich ancient garbage heaps in the Fayum and to the outskirts of Alexandria, where hellenistic grammarians arranged her strophes in the grouped lines still used today. There we will discover many books of Sappho's, as we have found the books of the gnostic Nag Hammadi Library in Egypt and the scriptures of the Dead Sea Scrolls in nearby Syria. And if we do not find more Sappho, what we have left will still be an intelligible constellation of sparkling fragments filling the heavens from the Great Bear down to the Southern Cross.

Europe's first woman poet combined amazing metaphor with candid passion. But being a woman, she wrote from her dubiously privileged position as a minor outsider in a busy male society. Outside the main business of the world—war, politics, remunerative work—Sappho could speak with feeling of her own world: her apprehension of stars and orchards, the troubles and summits of love, the cycles of life and death, and she chatted with Afroditi. She wrote, giving the impression of complete involvement, though even in her most intensely self-revealing poems her words have the jarring strength of detachment and accuracy. She wrote as one might speak, if one could speak in ordinary but perfectly cadenced speech. And suddenly we hear her, half-destroyed, revealing:

> I convulse, am greener than grass
> and feel my mind slip as I go
> 	close to death.

In another poem she is one of the speakers:

> Honestly I wish I were dead.
> When she left me she wept

profusely and told me,
"Oh how we've suffered in all this.
Psapfo, I swear I go unwillingly."

And I answered her,
"Be happy, go and remember me,
you know how we worshiped you."

At times, as in the interior conversations of the English metaphysical poet George Herbert, we are the poet. We become Sappho as she is talking with her friend Atthis or, in the famous ode to Afroditi, conversing almost fiercely with her ally the love goddess. In each case she uses the device of speech in poetry to achieve both close intimacy and objectifying distance. We discover a Sappho who is a wholly distinctive personality as opposed to a voice construed by thematic and prosodic convention. Though clearly descending from a tradition of earlier singers, she is never other than herself. Her contemporary could be Constantine Cavafy, for time does not separate their use of conversation and the recollection of past happiness, or the objective and overpowering confessional voice of these two poets of modernity. Line by line, with relentless and sly frankness and outrage, they construct the biography of a voice.

By contrast, Homer, the first man in Western literary history, is but a shadow in his own poetry. By some he is considered to be two Homers, one of the *Iliad* and one of the *Odyssey*, and by others, an editor whose composite voice combines elements of a bardic tradition. Sappho, despite scanty and often mythical biographical tradition, emerges as a realized figure through her poems. Homer was of the epic-heroic tradition, but it took a lyric age to produce the first major woman lyric poet. Or more justly, we can say that Sappho, along with Archilochos, who lived in the early part of the seventh century B.C.E, created the lyric age of antiquity. She talks, laughs, insults, speaks with irony or despair. As Longinos* tells us, she knows how to assemble details from true life to give us the lightning force of sublimity. We find such ecstatic transcendence in later poets, notably in the Persian Sufi poets and the English metaphysical poets, and in the mystico-erotic poems of Saint John of the Cross. But Sappho also conveys a different intensity—easy, spare, and piercing—in the meeting of two lovers, as in this very mutilated fragment, "Behind a Laurel Tree":

You lay in wait
behind a laurel tree

and everything
was sweeter

women
wandering

I barely heard
darling soul

such as I now am
you came

beautiful
in your garments

We know Sappho more intimately than any other ancient poet, with the possible exception of Catullus, who was enthralled by Sappho's poetry, imitated and translated her, and addressed his lover and muse in his poems as "Lesbia." She has permitted us to overhear her longing and intelligence, her humor and anger, and her perception of beauty. Her conversations

---

* Many scholars now call Longinos, the first-century author of *On the Sublime*, by the name Pseudo-Longinos to distinguish him from Cassius Longinos, a third-century author who through the nineteenth century was incorrectly believed to have composed this major treatise.

have the naturalness of a storyteller improvising in formal verse.* Though her poetry, with the exception of two complete poems,† survives only as fragments, her emerging portrait is as precise and profound as a Vermeer or a Goya. Yet that fresh image exists only as these fragments (some substantial), not at all in the unreliable testimonia, all from at least a century after her death.

A few essential facts can be drawn from external sources—where she was born, her approximate lifetime, a possible exile around 600 B.C.E., and that her fame as a lyric poet exceeded all others in Greek and Latin antiquity. As for her looks, character, family history, her profession and lifestyle, the abundant assertions in later writing are contradictory and mythical, and often no more than pleasant aphoristic gossip. Her father's names are multiple; her husband's name, Kerkylas; someone by the name Kleis is probably her daughter or possibly a favorite young friend. But these uncertainties are what we have. Ovid's *Letters of the Heroines*, 15, on Sappho and Phaon, is beautiful and fantastic and has nothing to do with Sappho other than that its tale reveals and celebrates the poet's enduring fame. I regret that I cannot read about the poets from Lesbos as one can about the lives of such extraordinary figures as Plotinos, Plato, and Pindar. But the absence of contemporary

---

* Some of those forms that she invented one could not see on papyrus as lineated verse, because the words were jammed together to save space. Those distinctions of lines and stanzas were the work of hellenistic rhetoricians in Alexandria centuries later.

† One of these two poems, fragment 58, was first published in 1922, but this was only a partial translation, based on an incomplete Greek fragment. The complete version of the poem—so far as we can tell—was published in 2004 after the discovery of a third century B.C.E. papyrus found in the Cologne University archives. Martin. L. West first published the find in Greek alone in the *Zeitschrift für Papyrologie und Epigraphik* 151 (2005), 1–9, and in Greek along with his English translation in the *Times Literary Supplement* (June 21, 2005, 1).

information should not trouble. The world's best-known writer, Shakespeare, wrote in a century of extensive documentation, but his portrait derives only from what may be guessed from the poems and plays and a history of the folio editions. Yet Sappho and William Shakespeare do very well, largely concealed from media fact and chronology but resonating in perfect pitch in their verse.

Sappho was born on Lesbos, an island in the Aigaion Sea a few miles off the coast of Asia Minor. Lesbos was then, as it is today, an island of grains, grapes, redolent orchards, and salt flats, spotted with five coastal cities that each commanded its harbor from a rocky acropolis. Greece is a country of light and sea rock—its source of beauty and too little farmland—and shows off its few precious valleys and plains of fertile land, along with its many hills and mountains, which are often terraced for wheat and olive trees up to their steep tops. Lesbos was unusual in having largely tillable terrain, along with its salt flats, dry hills then wooded, and a three-thousand-foot mountain called Olympos, after the traditional abode of the gods in Thessaly. It was known in ancient times for its grains, fruit trees, and, above all, the large valleys of olive groves. In twenty-six hundred years the island has probably changed very little in its village architecture and landscape. As one should know Baeza and Soria to understand Antonio Machado, or Vermont and New Hampshire to know Robert Frost, so there is no better way to know the images of Sappho's poetry than to see today the light, sea, and land of Mytilini, ancient Lesbos.*

---

* Mytilini was the major polis of ancient Lesbos. It is now the name of both the capital and the island. On modern maps, "Lesbos" often appears in parentheses and in modern Greek remains as an elegant synonym for "Mytilini" the island.

The biographical tradition of Sappho begins after her death and is a mixture of possible fact, contradiction, malice, and myth. Virtually all the testimonia are found in later grammarians, commentators, and historians such as Strabon, Athinaios, Herodotos, and Suidas (*The Suda Lexicon*). From all this at least some statements of probable truth may be made. Sappho's birthplace in Lesbos was either Eressos or Mytilini; in any case, it was in Mytilini that she spent most of her life. She was born ca. 630 B.C.E. Her name in Attic Greek (the language of Athens and of the bulk of ancient Greek literature) was Sappho (Σαπφώ), by which she is known, but in her native Aiolic she called herself Psapfo (Ψάπφω). She wrote as she spoke, and the speech of Lesbos was Aiolic Greek. In this work I predominately use *Sappho*, her Attic name, to refer to the poet. In the poems, however, I have preserved her own Aiolic spelling, *Psapfo*.

Her father's name was given as Skamandronymos, but it also appears as Skamandros, Simon, Euminos, Ierigyios, Etarhos, Ekrytos, Simos, and Kamon. Her mother's name was Kleis. Some suggest—and some deny—that she married a rich merchant from Andros named Kerkylas, who may have been the father of her daughter, Kleis. She had two brothers, perhaps three: Haraxos, Larihos, and possibly the more shadowy Eurygios. Several poems speak disapprovingly of Haraxos, a young man who paid for voyages abroad by trading wine from his estates and who had spent large sums of family money to buy the freedom in Egypt of a courtesan named Doriha. Larihos was a public cupbearer in Mytilini. We know nothing of Eurygios, if indeed he existed. As for Sappho's personal appearance, there were no statues, coins, or vase paintings until long after her death. But she was frequently referred to as the "lovely Sappho," and with the same authority she was described as short, dark, and ugly, "like a nightingale with misshapen wings enfolding a tiny body." These are the words of the scholiast on Lucian's *Portraits*. Yet the same Lucian, referring to her person, calls Sappho "the delicious glory of the Lesbians." In a poem ascribed to Plato from the *Greek Anthology* (or *Palatine Anthology*), she is called the "tenth Muse." What are certainly Plato's words are in the *Phaidros*, in which he has Socrates speak of her as "the beautiful Sappho." In this, Plato was reflecting at least one contemporary belief in her feminine beauty, and in the existing statues and coins the "nightingale with misshapen wings" is depicted with the idealized features and beauty of Afroditi.

The evidence of her activities is no more conclusive. Sappho lived during the reigns of three tyrants in Lesbos: Melanhros, Myrsilos, and Pittakos the Sage. When she was young, it appears that she and her family went, for political reasons while under Myrsilos, to the Lesbian hill city of Pyrrha, and later, about 600 B.C.E., to Syracuse in Sicily, probably in the time of Pittakos. To have left for political reasons implies that her family was important in city affairs. As for her own social position, there is no question that her wealth and class distinction gave her privilege and, largely, immunity from male domination. Her relationship with men was not, at least in the surviving verse, political or societal but was, rather, a question of affection and sexuality. In perhaps her most famous poem, fragment 31, she is pitted as an outsider woman, for the love of another woman, against an impossibly superior competitor, a man who in her eyes seems godlike and completely excludes her from the erotic agon. In this attitude she differs from her aesthetic cousin, the Shulamite of the Song of Songs, who is one of the earliest voices to speak eloquently and powerfully from a woman's vantage point. The Shulamite celebrates erotic love and protests against the night guards of the city who have beaten her, "those guardians of the walls." Sappho is at least free from the bullying of such "night guards," but is nevertheless confined by her sex to a parallel world of aristocratic women.

This should not suggest, however, that Sappho and other women were viewed by men, or viewed themselves, as equals. Although the Greeks did honor nine male poets—Pindar being first among them—we find Aristotle stating superciliously in the *Rhetoric* (1398b): "The Mytilinians honored Sappho although she was a woman." But with all the hits and misses, Sappho is universally honored as the foremost lyric poet of Greek and Roman antiquity.

The women mentioned in Sappho's poems as companions are Anaktoria, Atthis, and Gongyla; she loved them passionately and shared catalogs of happiness with them, which she recalls with pain and pleasure after they have left her. Other friends are Mika and Telesippa and Anagora; she was angry with Gorgo and Andromeda, who had left her to become her rivals. But of the widely held theory of Ulrich von Wilamowitz-Moellendorff and others that her relationship to all these women was that of high priestess in a cult-association (*thiasos*), or in a young lady's academy of manners, the most one can say is that she was probably known as a teacher of young women. As for using her position of teacher at any level (and surely "cult" is a stretch) as a means of explaining away her homoerotic poems, this is unpleasant nonsense and traditional bigotry, and has no basis in the ancient biographical tradition and no support in the existing remains of her poems. Unfortunately, the cover-up theory, born of moral desire to conceal Sappho's gay romances, remained dominant until the mid-twentieth century.*

---

* Just how prevalent the disguisement was, was proved to me one day in June of 1962, in Burgos, Spain. I had been working in the archives of the Spanish poet Manuel Machado, brother of Antonio Machado, to find information about don Antonio. I came on a postcard to Manuel sent to him in the early 1930s by Miguel de Unamuno. Unamuno was a foremost Spanish

The ancient commentators have also told us that there were really two Sapphos—one a poet and one a prostitute who also wrote poems—or that Sappho herself was a prostitute, and Ovid recounts the legend that she threw herself from the Leukadian Cliff out of love for the ferryman Phaon. It should be remembered when considering these more extravagant tales about Sappho and her family that there were perhaps thirteen plays dealing with Sappho in later Attic comedy, and that by then she had become a stock figure on the Athenian stage. It was on the stage, her modern apologists contend, that the black legend of Sappho originated. The black legend extended to her husband, Kerkylas, whose name only appears in testimonia found in the late Byzantine *Suda*. The same wild Aristophanic imagination and comic nastiness that portrayed Socates as a fool standing on clouds and made Sappho into a babbling stage clown surely took shots at her husband, Kerkylas.

As we are told, Sappho's husband was from the island of Andros, meaning "man." In "Kerkylas" one can hear the word

---

novelist, poet, and philosopher, and also a classical scholar, maverick journalist, and then rector (president) of the University of Salamanca. In intellectual thought, Unamuno was and remains a grand world author, admired for his novelistic innovations that anticipate later postmodernism. His most famous exchange with history occurred in late August of 1936, when Francisco Franco's army took over Salamanca and its medieval university. At a meeting with the generals in his office, Unamuno denounced them, saying, "Vencerán tal vez pero no convencerán" (You may win but not convince). The response was shouts of "¡Muera la inteligencia!" (Let the intelligentsia die!). The philosopher was placed under house arrest, where he remained till his death. Despite all of his enlightened academic, creative, and courageous baggage, Unamuno wrote in his card to Manuel Machado that he had recently been rereading his Greek Sappho, "not the one of the infamous reputation but the true Sappho in the poems." Unamuno's message was that whoever really knew Greek knew that Sappho was *not* a lesbian.

kerkís, meaning "rod," "peg," or "weaver's spindle," which has led some scholars to speculate that both Sappho's husband's name and his origin were an invention and "indecent pun" from one of the many later comedies—such as the six comedies entitled *Sappho,* the five entitled *The Leucadian,* or two entitled *Phaon*—all lost plays known to us only by their titles, but in which Sappho was a target for lampoon. So, according to ancient comedic reasoning, "Kerkylas of Andros" yielded "Penis of Man," or, in more futsy academic jargon, "Prick from the Isle of Man."*

Sappho is credited with certain technical innovations. She is said to have been the first to use the *pectis* (a kind of harp), and to have invented the Mixolydian mode and the Sapphic stanza, which was imitated by Horace and Catullus. Sappho was not the first Lesbian to contribute innovations to Greek poetry. Before her were the semilegendary poets Arion, inventor of the dithyramb, and Leshes, author of the *Little Iliad,* and then Terpandros, who invented and wrote poetry for the seven-string lyre, of whom we have four small and doubtful fragments, the earliest examples of lyric poetry in Greece. Sappho's Lesbian contemporary Alkaios wrote in Alcaics (quatrains in tetrameters), which were also imitated by Horace and other Latin poets.

There is good reason to believe that Sappho was a prolific writer. We do not know how she recorded her work—whether on papyrus, on wooden tablets overlaid with wax, or orally through song—but centuries later, when the Alexandrian grammarians arranged her work according to meter into nine books, the first book contained 1,320 lines (330 four-line stanzas in sapphics—three eleven-syllable lines followed by a five-syllable

---

* See David A. Campbell, ed., *Greek Lyric Poetry: A Selection* (London: Macmillan, 1967), 5 n. 4.

line; in reality, Sappho used many metric forms, not only the prosodic form that carries her name).* Judging from this, we may suppose that the nine books contained a very extensive opus. Her work was well known and well preserved in antiquity. We have Athinaios's claim in the third century c.e. that he knew all of Sappho's lyrics by heart. But the best indication, perhaps, of the general availability of her works in the classical age lies in the number of quotations from her poems by grammarians, even late into Roman times, which suggests that both commentator and reader had ready access to the corpus of the work being quoted.

Of the more than five hundred poems by Sappho, we have today about two thousand lines that fit into intelligible fragments, and these come from no single collected copy but are pieced together from many sources: from the scholia of ancient grammarians to the mummy wrappings in Egyptian tombs. Plato's entire work has survived virtually intact, having been both popular with and approved by pagan and Christian alike. Sappho's work did not lack popularity. As Ovid put it, "What did Sappho of Lesbos teach but how to love women?" (*Lesbia quid docuit Sappho nisi amare puellas?*) But nonetheless, she did not always win approval.

To the church mind, Sappho represented the culmination of moral laxity, and her work was treated with extreme disapproval. About 380 c.e., Saint Gregory of Nazianzos, bishop of Constantinople, ordered the burning of Sappho's writings

---

* The above description of the sapphic is crude, omitting all reference to length of syllables (short and long) and irregularities. For more see Denys Page's "Appendix on Metres" in *Sappho and Alcaeus: An Introduction to the Study of Ancient Lesbian Poetry* (Oxford: Oxford University Press, 1959); *The Meters of Greek and Latin Poetry* by James W. Halporn, Martin Ostwald, and Thomas G. Rosenmeyer (Indianapolis: Bobbs Merrill, 1963); and the Metrical Guide by William E. McCulloh at the end of this book.

wherever found. She had already been violently attacked as early as 180 C.E. by the Assyrian ascetic Tatian: "Sappho was a whorish woman, love-crazy, who sang about her own licentiousness."*

Then in 391 a mob of Christian zealots partially destroyed Ptolemy Soter's classical library in Alexandria. The often repeated story of the final destruction of this famous library by the Arab general 'Amr ibn al-'Āṣ and Caliph 'Umar I is now rejected by historians. Again we hear that in 1073 Sappho's writings were publicly burned in Rome and Constantinople by order of Pope Gregory VII. Until late in the eleventh century, however, quotations from Sappho still appeared in the works of grammarians, suggesting that copies of her poems were still preserved. We will never know how many poems by Sappho were destroyed in April 1204 during the terrible pillage of Constantinople by the Venetian knights of the Fourth Crusade, or by the Ottoman Turks at the fall of Byzantium in 1453.

But apart from official hostility, Sappho's works suffered equally from the general decline of learning in the early Middle Ages and the consequent anger of oxidizing time upon neglected manuscripts. It is probable that some of her work was lost in about the ninth century when classical texts, preserved in uncial script, were selected and recopied in modern letters. No single collection of her poems, in whole or in part, survived the medieval period. Nevertheless, in the Renaissance, Sappho came back into light. Italian scholars found the essays *On the Sublime* by Longinos and *On Literary Composition* by Dionysios of Halikarnassos, which contain two of Sappho's most important poems: fragment 31, "Seizure," and the complete ode to Afroditi (fragment 1, "Prayer to Afroditi"). Every

* *Oratio ad graecos*, 53.

stanza, line, and isolated word by Sappho that appeared in the works of other Greek and Latin writers was assembled, including indirect poems, that is, summaries or retellings of her poems.*

Very few fragments of original papyrus manuscripts have survived in continental Greece,† but in parts of rainless Egypt in the Fayum, an oasis semidetached from the Nile Valley near Krokodilopolis, important papyrus manuscripts with poems by Sappho were discovered in 1879. The Egyptian expeditions by the English scholars B. P. Grenfell and A. S. Hunt, beginning in 1897, yielded a wealth of material. In addition to important

---

* In the last few years our means of deciphering both papyri and parchment texts have dramatically increased as a result of X-rays and infrared technology. At the Stanford Linear Accelerator Center at Stanford University, a particle accelerator is being used to read a hitherto unreadable tenth-century palimpsest containing a 174-page book of the mathematician Archimedes hidden below a Christian prayer book. The original writing was erased in order to record a Christian prayer book. By shooting X-rays at the parchment, the iron in the ink of the "erased" ancient text glows, revealing a now perfectly legible mathematic treatise under the later prayer book.

A parallel technological breakthrough is being used to decipher the literary elements of the some four hundred thousand Oxyrhynchus papyri fragments. Through multispectral imaging based on satellite imaging, the faded ink on ancient papyri comes clearly into view. English and American scientists and scholars have already deciphered lines from Sophocles' lost play *Epigonoi* (The Progeny), three pages in elegiac meter by the seventh-century lyric poet Archilochos, and works by Euripides, Hesiod, and Lucian. There is realistic hope that in coming years the amount of significant ancient texts, including early Gnostic and Christian scripture, may be increased by more than twenty percent. Hopefully, this translation of Sappho's works will soon be outdated when new strophes from the popular Lesbian poet are revealed. For extensive information, see POxy (Oxyrhynchus Online) at www.papyrology.ox.ac.uk.

† In 1961, for the first time, a cache of eight original papyri, in poor condition, was found in continental Greece at Dervani (Lagada). See Herbert Hunger, "Papyrusfund in Griechenland," *Chronique d'Egypte* (Brussels) 37, no. 74 (July 1961).

---

poems by Sappho, parts of four plays of Menandros were found in a refuse heap near Afroditopolis; at Oxyrhynhos, Alkman's maiden-song choral ode, the first in Greek literature, and twenty odes by Bacchylides were discovered. Bacchylides ceased to be simply a name and became again a major poet of antiquity, rivaling Pindar.

But above all, the range of Sappho's work was dramatically expanded. The precious papyri had been used as papier-mâché in mummy wrappings. Unfortunately, many were torn in vertical strips, and as a result the Sappho fragments are mutilated at the beginning or end of lines, if not in the middle. The mummy makers of Egypt transformed much of Sappho into columns of words, syllables, or single letters, and so made her poems look, at least typographically, like Apollinaire's or e. e. cummings's shaped poems.

The miserable state of many of the texts has produced surprising qualities. So many words and phrases are elliptically connected in montage structure that chance destruction has delivered us pieces of strophes that breathe experimental verse. Her time-scissored work is not quite language poetry, but a more joyful cousin of the eternal avant-garde, which is always and never new. So Sappho is ancient and, for a hundred reasons, modern.

Ezra Pound goes back full circle when he "antiques" the form of a poem in order to make it resemble a vertical strip of a Sappho papyrus. His brief poem "Papyrus," addressed to Gongyla, reads:

Spring . . .
Too long . . .
Gongula . . .

But Sappho aces him with an impeccable strip in which plenitude resides in the ruins of her script:

Return, Gongyla

A deed
your lovely face

if not, winter
and no pain

I bid you, Abanthis,
take up the lyre
and sing of Gongyla as again desire
floats around you

the beautiful. When you saw her dress
it excited you. I'm happy.
The Kypros-born once
blamed me

for praying
this word:
I want

In her minimalist Imagist period, H.D., and her descen-
dents in the Black Mountains, learned from Sappho, copied
her absences, and found themselves through her losses. Wil-
liam Carlos Williams translated her and Robert Creeley and
the Brazilian concrete poets were her immediate kin. But de-
spite this *parenté d'esprit* that truly helped generate our mod-
ernist movements, the price of the unwitting modernization
of Sappho scripture, through the random damage of her po-
ems, has resulted in the tantalizing loss of intelligibility of
hundreds of her fragments, not to mention the disappearance
of most of her work.

The cost was also high to the English and German schol-
ars who undertook the labor of unraveling the damaged pa-
pyri (both literally and figuratively). The German scholar
Friedrich Blass, who first deciphered important poems by

Sappho in these Fayum manuscripts, lost the use of his eyes, and Bernard P. Grenfell, the explorer and pioneer editor of *Oxyrhynchus Papyri*, during his intense labors for a while lost his mind. Most hurtful to Sappho were the majority of her defenders from the seventeenth to the early twentieth century, who in their eagerness to clean up Sappho's act, to create a morally sound "divine Sappho," quite lost their perspective of the poet and hopelessly muddled the poet's life with the poems.

While a thousand years of bigotry destroyed the greater part of Sappho's poetry, the zeal of her later defenders, from Anne Lefebvre Dacier in 1682 to Ulrich von Wilamowitz-Moellendorff, Bruno Snell, and C. M. Bowra,* to rehabilitate her moral character has not helped the poet's cause, nor has it contributed to our understanding of her work. It is no less than astonishing how otherwise temperate scholars became outraged and imaginatively unobjective at the slightest suggestions by others of moral frivolity on Sappho's part. Not Sappho's poems but Middle and New Comedy and Horace and Ovid are accused of instigating the black legend. Several arguments are offered and reiterated to justify her love poems to other women. The dominating cure was the *thiasos* remedy: since Sappho was a priestess and the head of a circle of young women, these poems did not mean literally what they say; her love poems to women were epithalamia written for ceremonial purposes; the poems castigating her brother Haraxos for his affair with Doriha prove her own high virtue; Alkaios once addressed her as *agya* (holy or chaste); she came from a noble and highly respectable Lesbian family. The arguments read like a brief—in an unnecessary trial.

In the nineteenth century the denial of Sappho's homosexu-

---

* Bowra modifies his defense of Sappho's "purity" in the 1961 edition of his *Greek Lyric Poetry,* by which time fellow scholars took a new line, acknowledging that Sappho's poems were indeed homoerotic.

ality prevailed. There were exceptions to an illusory interpretation of her poems, but these were not apparently heeded. We find some notable exceptions in England and a tragic one in the instance of Charles Baudelaire, who paid bitterly for his candor. Perhaps the clearest statement regarding Sappho's sexuality appears in William Mure of Caldwell's *A Critical History of the Language and Literature of Antient Greece*. While the Scottish classicist condemns Sappho for her "scandalous history" and her "taste for impure intercourse, which forms so foul a blot on the Greek national character," he pooh-poohs the standard notion of Sappho's higher "purity" and insists that her Lesbian female "association" was nothing less than the "pursuit of love and pleasure." He writes, commenting sharply on fragment 31:

> In several places, Sappho addresses certain of her female associates in terms of no less voluptuous passion than those employed towards her male objects of adoration. In one passage, equal in power and nearly equal in length to the ode to Venus already cited, her ardour is inflamed by the sight of a rival, a male rival it may be remarked, participating, however slightly, in the privileges to which she herself claimed an exclusive right. She describes it as "a bliss equal to that of the gods to sit by the music of her voice, and gaze on her fascinating smile." At the same time, in anger against her male rival she feels "mortification and jealousy."*

In his modern "right on" commentary, William Mure notes, "If Sappho did *not* mean or feel what she has expressed in the

* William Mure of Caldwell, *A Critical History of the Language and Literature of Antient Greece*, 2nd ed., vol. 3 (London: Longman, Brown, Green, and Longmans, 1854), pp. 315–16.

passage above, then the most brilliant extant specimens of her muse become comparatively unmeaning rhapsodies; if she *did* so feel, her sentiments were not those of maternal tenderness of sisterly friendship."

A generation later, John Addington Symonds (who had "shocked" Walt Whitman in a letter sent to the American poet, assuming their common passion for men) speaks of Sappho's homoeroticism. He slightly tempers his view of Sappho as a practicing homosexual by contrasting her "sating of the senses" with the cruder voluptuousness of Persian or Arabic art. He writes, "All is so rhythmically and sublimely ordered in the poems of Sappho that supreme art lends solemnity and grandeur to the expression of unmitigated passion."* He then laments the ruin of her literary remains: "The world has suffered no greater literary loss than the loss of Sappho's poems."

In mid- and late-nineteenth-century France, official morality and hypocrisy reigned with respect to Sappho's lesbianism. While by the end of the century, there was a fad and rash of lesbian novels and memoirs published under the guise of being "newly found novels by the poetess Sappho," when Charles Baudelaire published his *Les Fleurs du mal* in 1857, *Le Figaro* condemned the book as "the putrescence of the human heart." In large part because of his inclusion of six poems concerning Sappho and *les femmes damnées*, the author and his publisher Auguste Poulet-Malassis were dragged to court, convicted, and heavily fined. The six "lesbian" poems were banned from the book, and Poulet-Malassis was sent to prison. An appeal to the empress Eugénie resulted in the reduction of Baudelaire's fines. Only in 1949 was the ban on the immoral poems officially lifted.

It is extraordinary that until mid-twentieth century the

---

* John Addington Symmonds, *Studies of the Greek Poets* (London: Smith, Elder, & Co., 1873), p. 173.

myth of Sappho's chaste love remained standard fare. In this cover-up there is an exact parallel with the confused and disturbed denunciations of those who dared to suggest that William Shakespeare was stained by the abnormal emotions of Greek love. Such folly was expressed only by weak critics blind to the poet's metaphysical message and spiritual convention. Oscar Wilde was an obvious exception. He loved the *Sonnets*, he tells us in letters, and he theorized that the young man who received Shakespeare's relentless ardor was actually "a wonderful lad" named Willie Hews, "a boy actor in his plays." On the third and last day of his famous trial of "gross indecency" for a homosexual act in 1895, Wilde invoked the *Sonnets* in his defense, a declaration that served to deepen his legal guilt.

In *Shakespeare's Sonnets*, the editor, Katherine Duncan-Jones, addresses the almost universal dissemblance of Shakespeare's homosexual passions. Without sympathy she describes W. H. Auden's complex manner of reading *Sonnets*, saying that interpretation becomes "entwined with the personality (and sexuality) of the critic, as well as his or her cultural location." She writes:

> This is the case of W. H. Auden. Though anyone with a knowledge of Auden's biography might expect him to celebrate and endorse the homoerotic character of 1–126, he was absolutely determined not to do so, at least publicly. In his 1964 Signet edition Auden claimed—as G. Wilson Knight had done— that the primary experience explored in *Sonnets* was "mystical," and he was extremely scathing about putative readers of homosexual inclinations who might be "determined to secure our Top-Bard as a patron saint of the Homointern." Yet his public adoption of this position seems to have been a characteristic instance of Auden's cowardice, for later in 1964 he

confessed to friends that a public account of Shakespeare (evidently equated by Auden with the speaker in *Sonnets*) as homosexual "won't do just yet." Perhaps Auden was referring to the changes in legislation then under discussion: Parliament finally decriminalized homosexual acts between consenting adults in July 1967.*

By contrast with Auden's prudence, the Alexandrian poet Constantine Cavafy (1863–1933) in the early 1900s fully presented his homosexuality in his poems, which, however, he printed only privately, to give to friends. Despite candor in verse, he too faced the reality of the impossible public plight of gays. Though he was in his lifetime known as the foremost poet in the Greek language and T. S. Eliot published his poems in 1924 in his *The Criterion*, Cavafy could not permit a collection of his own poems, carefully ordered by his own hand, to be published while he was alive. We hear his own moving statement about public acknowledgment in his prescient "Hidden Things":

> From all I did and all I said
> let them not try to find out who I was.
> An obstacle stood before me and transformed
> my acts and my way of life.
> An obstacle stood before me and stopped me
> so often from what I was going to say.
> My most unnoticed acts
> and my most veiled writings—
> only from these will they know me.
> But maybe it's not worth it to devote
> so much care and effort to knowing me.

* Katherine Duncan-Jones, *Shakespeare's Sonnets* (London: Arden Shakespeare, 1997), 80–81.

Later—in a more perfect society—
someone made like me
will certainly appear and act freely.* [1908]

In England and America Sir Denys Page was the first major academic scholar to oppose all this posturing about Sappho's sexuality. Page, who with Edgar Lobel has produced the most authoritative edition of Sappho's works, chose to look at the texts and found that the poems gave no support whatsoever to the arguments. Page contends that Sappho was not a high priestess; only a small portion of her poems might be considered epithalamia; and Sappho herself, far from being a woman of unfailingly noble sentiments, was a common mortal concerned with common matters of love and jealousy. In deflating the contentions of her supporters, Page also deflates Sappho herself—not without a note of moral reproach.

I have spent some time reviewing the history of Sappho's usually violent encounter with the world, not because one must necessarily know something or anything about an author to appreciate the work, but because in Sappho's case the world has known—or assumed—too much, and this knowledge interferes with any fair appraisal of her poems. The question has been whether Sappho was indeed a lesbian in the sexual—and not just the geographical—sense of the word.

First, it should be stated that whatever Sappho was in her life has very little to do with the content of her poetry; whether she was indeed bisexual or merely ascetic like her contemporaries Jeremiah and Gautama Siddhartha will not change the meaning of her poems. It is not that an author's intention must be discounted, nor need we puristically fear the heresy of intentional fallacy or other critical sins, old and new, including

---

* The translation is by Aliki Barnstone in *The Collected Poems of C. P. Cavafy: A New Translation* (New York: W. W. Norton 2006), 36.

historiological snooping into her time and culture. Yet if the author's intention is meaningful, it must be seen through the text, through the lyrical speaker in the poem, and not merely from outside sources. In Sappho's case the problem is more rudimentary. Even if we could accept outside sources, there is, in fact, no reliable authority outside the poems themselves to explain the author's intended meaning in her many poems dealing with love.

Nonetheless, the preponderance of recent literary research assumes an authoritative understanding of her culture and historical times, which runs the same risks of blunder and uncertainty as in the work of earlier literary critics, including my old heroes C. M. Bowra and Denys Page. How helpful is the work of social historians in reading the poems of Sappho? As ever, there is much to be learned from serious investigation and much to be questioned. And new generations will question again. In these domains none of us is sinless, but as an amateur reader, I prefer the less serious approach that sees Sappho mainly through her work, and reads her work not as document but as art.

To find Sappho, then, the Sappho of the poems, we may look long at the poems themselves. One fragment is addressed to her daughter, Kleis. A few of them may have been addressed to men. The majority are love poems to women. They are passionate poems, self-critical, self-revealing, detached, and intense. If we are to believe what they say, we will conclude that the speaker in the poems experienced a physical passion for her beloved, with all the sexual implications that similar poems between men and women normally imply. (Much of the world's love poetry is homoerotic, and in ancient Greek poetry, the majority of love poems by known male poets, from Ibykos to Pindar, are addressed to other men.) To give the poems meanings that the texts do not support, for whatever moral motive, is to dilute Sappho's language and to weaken and falsify her work. Even though the remains of her oeuvre are scant, the poems should be allowed a plain reading of unimaginative literalness. "Uninterpreted" they speak for Sappho more directly and eloquently than the countertexts of her old defenders.

In the fragments we have left, only a few lines give details of physical love: "May you sleep on your tender girlfriend's breast." Many speak of her passions. Sappho's best-known love poem, "Seizure" (fragment 31), is an example of her precision, objectivity, and cumulative power. The poem is direct, self-revealing, yet detached and calmly accurate at the moment of highest fever. She begins with a statement of her pain at the sight of the man sitting near the woman she loves, who, because of his envied position, appears godlike to her; she recounts the physical symptoms of her passion for the woman; and with full intensity but without exaggeration, she uses the metaphor of green turning greener than grass to show her suffering, verging on death, because of a love not returned.

Seizure

To me he seems equal to gods,
the man who sits facing you
and hears you near as you speak
    softly and laugh

in a sweet echo that jolts
the heart in my ribs. Now
when I look at you a moment
    my voice is empty

and can say nothing as my tongue
cracks and slender fire races
under my skin. My eyes are dead
    to light, my ears

pound, and sweat pours over me.
I convulse, greener than grass
and feel my mind slip as I go
    close to death.

Yet I must suffer all, even poor

    The poem states a love relationship, but more, it states the
poet's agony when, consumed by love, she is unable to com-
pete with the rival—a man, a species with powers inaccessible
to her as a woman, and who therefore appears equal to a god.
She cannot reach the woman she loves. The woman affects her
with paralyzing force, and she can in no way escape, except
through words, from the solitude in which she is suddenly
enclosed. Her senses are agitated and fail her. She can no lon-
ger see, speak, or hear.
    As her bodily functions weaken, she moves close to death,
her analogue of the *via negativa*. The mystics would describe
this state as dying away from space and time. In Daoist termi-
nology, she is moving to the open country of emptiness. There,
as in Saint John of the Cross's dark sensory night of aridities,
she reaches momentary detachment from bodily senses, which
permits her to speak objectively of the symptoms of her pas-
sion. She too is "dying from love." And like those who have
had intense physical pain, at a certain threshold she becomes a
distant observer of herself. Unlike Saint John, however, the
night of purgation is not, at least in this fragment, the moment
before the joyful night (*la noche dichosa*) of illumination and
union.
    Sappho's desire is conveyed as a loss of self. She is exiled, as it
were, from her desire and remains in a darkness before death.
In Saint John this darkness is described as "withdrawal ecstasy."
In Sappho the movement from the self into an extraordinary

condition of void and separation results in a violent failure of the senses, a seizure, the ekstasis of negative ecstasy (of being elsewhere, but in the wrong place). For the mystics, the second stage is illumination, the discovery of a new self. However, in Sappho this second stage is blackness, the discovery of the loss of self. The catalog of symptoms of her seizure is a universal condition that finds expression in varying diction and metaphors, secular or religious, from Saint Teresa's interior castles and Andrew Marvell's entrapment in the garden to Marghanita Laski's medical analyses* and Jorge Guillén's passionate merging in the circle of light. Hers, however, is love's lightless inferno, without union and without the peace that follows union.

Unable to reach the object of her love, there is no fulfillment and no release except in the objectification of her passion in the poem. Yet in her poetry she does indeed reach the world, if not her beloved. Her words, used masterfully, make the reader one with the poet, to share her vision of herself. There is no veil between poet and reader. Here, as elsewhere in her art, Sappho makes the lyric poem a refined and precise instrument for revealing her intensely personal experience. As always, through the poems alone, we construct the true biography of voice. As mentioned earlier, in one poem in the *Greek Anthology*, Plato speaks of Sappho as the "tenth Muse." The ascription of the epigram to Plato, as of all thirty-seven poems ascribed to him, is shaky. What is certain is that these words reflect ancient opinion. Sappho's own expression of the continuity of her words appears in an astonishing line that neither contains silly phrases "worthy of a Muse" nor betrays any of the ambitious glitter and bay leaves in Petrarch's notion of

---

* For an interesting and full examination of the condition of transport, see Marghanita Laski, *Ecstasy: A Study of Some Secular and Religious Experiences* (Bloomington: Indiana University Press, 1962).

fame. Rather, the intimate voice, serenely ascertaining its future, is prophetic:

> Someone, I tell you, in another time,
> will remember us.

Sappho is remembered despite the multiple violations of time. The fragments of her poems contain the first Western examples of ecstasy, including the sublime, which the first-century Longinos recognized and preserved for us. They also include varieties of ekstasis briefly alluded to in these pages: the bliss of Edenic companionship, dancing under the moon, breakfasts in the grass; the whirlwind blast of love; the desolation and rage of betrayal; the seizure and paralysis before impossible love; and as all her ordinary senses fail, the movement near death—the ultimate negative ecstasy. Yet even when she has lost herself, her senses, her impossible love, Sappho is remembered. The diversity and clarity of her voice, the absolute candor, the amazing fresh authority of the poetry, whether in addressing a goddess, a Homeric marriage couple, the moon and stars, a sweet apple or mountain hyacinth, a lamb or cricket, a lover or companion, those qualities compelled in antiquity as they do today.

Ordering of the Texts with Respect to Chronology and Other Editions

The order of Sappho's poems in standard editions does not reflect chronology of composition or the author's age. It may, as in the work by Edgar Lobel and Denys Page, attempt to reflect Sappho's nine "books" or, given the losses, the remnants of her collections. Lobel and Page fragments 1 to 117 are presented as clearly by Sappho, and fragments 118 to 213 (none of the longer poems) follow under the title *Incerti libri*, meaning that they are of uncertain ascription. The actual order or grouping within the books is mostly unknown, since Sappho's hand is not there. They were accomplished in hellenistic times. This traditional presentation is thought to have been determined three centuries after Sappho by the Alexandrian scholars Aristophanes of Byzantium and Aristarchos of Samathrace, when her work was alive and well received.

In this edition the fragments have been ordered independently of their traditional numbering, under a logic that is a mixture of theme and implied chronology and event. Here, the poem number of the Greek source text generally follows the number established in *Poetarum Lesbiorum Fragmenta*, edited by Lobel and Page (abbreviated here as LP), and the Loeb Classical Library *Sappho and Alcaeus*, edited and translated by David A. Campbell. The latter normally has the same numbering as Lobel and Page, though the Greek texts differ. So unless otherwise noted, the numbering standing alone refers to the Lobel and Page Greek text.

My reading of letters and words tends to be closer to the more recent editions by Eva-Maria Voigt, Max Treu, and Campbell than to Lobel and Page. Where the Greek text does not follow the numbering of Lobel and Page, I indicate in the Sources which other text has been followed, usually Campbell. When Campbell ascribes a poem to Sappho that Lobel and Page ascribe to Alkaios, I also follow Campbell, who always notes the Lobel and Page ascription. I have also consulted the Denys Page transcriptions in *Sappho and Alcaeus*. When one of Sappho's fragments is not in Lobel and Page but is found in Campbell, Ernest Diehl (*Anthologia Lyrica Graeca*, vol. 1), Voigt (*Sappho et Alcaeus*), or Treu, who adds his own material to earlier Diehl, these differences in judgment are indicated. The judgments refer to texts of uncertain ascription—whether to Sappho, Alkaios, or to a late false attribution—and are indicated by "incert."

While the numbering follows Lobel and Page unless otherwise noted, the Greek is a composite based on Lobel and Page, and also Voigt and Diehl, but predominantly on Campbell because of his selectivity. In Campbell the sigla, or scholarly markings, are at a minimum, making the Greek text more pleasant and reader-friendly. Campbell normally leaves out words and lines that he views as unintelligible.

With respect to Campbell's English renderings, I have found his strictly prose versions excellent and a benefit to all readers. I would use the word "interpretation" to describe them, because the Greek is so uncertain. He has also chosen, with exceptions, to reproduce those lines of Greek that lend themselves to intelligible translation and then his guesses in reading uncertain letters and words are chaste and selective. Even as a gloss and dictionary they are invaluable, and more so than the existing beautiful poetic versions.

The measure for determining which of the diverse texts I draw from for each fragment has been their intelligibility for translation purposes. When unintelligible, the Greek is usually not given, which means that in a number of poems many lines are omitted (Campbell generally follows this practice), and hence in this edition the Greek generally matches the English as parallel texts.

Sources and Titles

In the Sources, Notes, and Commentary section, I provide bibliographical source information for the poems translated in this edition as well as ancient commentary related to the poems. Sappho's fragments survive in papyri or in ancient commentaries. For almost each fragment, if an ancient commentary exists—prosodic, grammatical, or literary—it is provided here. First given is the ancient bibliographical source; any ancient commentary appears next in quotation marks. My own commentary sometimes follows.

The source and formal commentary normally provide the

material from which the poem's title comes. Sappho did not title her poems. I have made use of the "free line," which is a poem's title, in order to give the reader information found in the source and commentary, or derived from a close study of a difficult or evasive fragment. A simple example: In the one-line fragment 54, the subject noun of the verb is missing in the Greek text. It reads: ". . . came out of heaven dressed in a purple cape." However, the lexicographer Pollux, in whose *Vocabulary* this line is cited and thereby preserved, states that Sappho is describing Eros. Hence we know the subject of the verb and have an informative title: "Eros." Some translators add titles, others do not. I add them because a fine title can offer an immediate smooth opening into a mutilated text. It is preferable to obtrusive footnotes and gives the reader clues before turning to the back of the book. If it illumines, good. Then the reader can choose, or not choose, to look for more end-of-book information.

In the event of translation there are many ways to reach a Sappho, and the history of ancient literatures globally, alas, abounds in literary remnants. Titles help give them sense. In what seems to be the most recent version of many of Sappho's fragments, in striking re-creations Sherod Santos provides appropriate titles. Mary Barnard gives titles. Anne Carson's elegant versions do not, but the poet and classical scholar more than makes up for any information gap with her abundant and fascinating endnotes and commentary on the poems.

Greek Words in English

The transliteration of proper nouns and common nouns from one language to another is universally transitional and vexing. One cannot be entirely consistent without being silly and awkward. Who is happy when the English render Livorno, Amedeo Modigliani's birthplace, as Leghorn? However, there is radical change. In transliterating Chinese into English, in a generation we have gone from standard English Wade-Giles to standard Pinyin. At the beginning Pinyin was shocking and difficult. Now Pinyin is de rigueur for scholarship, dictionaries, and newspapers, though it remains a difficult replacement. Some frequently used words in common speech have quickly yielded to Pinyin, such as *Peking*, now rendered as *Beijing*.* *Canton* (*Kwangchow* in Wade-Giles) is on the way to becoming *Guangzhou*, but that change is challenging.

Rendering the Greek alphabet in English is more challenging because there are so many interests that have imposed their spelling on Greek as it has slipped into other languages. Latin Rome conquered Greece and translated Greek gods into Roman ones. Artemis became Diana, Zeus yielded to Jupiter or Jove. Greek words were transliterated into Latin letters, not always close in sound or feeling. English and the Romance languages have followed the practice of Latinizing Greek names while Germany and Eastern Europe keep closer to the Greek.

While the ancient Alexandrian scholars preserved and fashioned Sappho, ordering and editing her poetry, since Horace and Quintilian there has been war between "grammarians" and "libertines" over the nature of translation itself, between *fidus interpres*, which the Latin writers mocked, and literary re-creation and imitation. In modern times the soft war goes on between translation as a literary art or a classroom language test, which is revealed in spelling. The combatants regularly have seats in the academy, and victory

---

* In Wade-Giles, if one knew the rules, which neither people nor dictionaries did, *Peking* was supposed to be pronounced *Beijing* because the unvoiced consonants *p* and *k* were to be voiced. Fat chance. Only when ungainly Pinyin took over did we have a clue about transcribing Mandarin (*putonghua*) into English. We are still stuck with *Tao* instead of *Dao*, though not for long.

depends on which audience and publisher receives and acclaims them. As for the gods and their IDs, outside Romance tongues the Greek gods have regained their identity. As for the transcription of names, unlike Chinese where one power has enforced its system (notwithstanding holdouts in Taiwan and Singapore), there is no single rule book for regulating transliteration. This free-for-all mode reflects language flux, which is always with us, no matter who is emperor.

With no absolutes on the horizon, what is happening now? Despite the minor brawls, much happened in the twentieth century to return us to equivalents resembling the Greek scripture (though James Joyce did not get the word when he dropped the bomb of *Ulysses*). My own perplexities on the *how* (and here the quandary is not art versus gloss but simply on how to record the change of signs between tongues) at least is typical, and in my weathercock self I spin with each puff of revelation. I have been tinkering with classical Greek for many decades along with Koine Greek and biblical Hebrew. When I undertook the translation of the New Testament, a book from Asia Minor, I chose to restore, as far as one can know, the original Hebrew, Aramaic, and Greek names so that a reader might observe that most of the figures in the scriptures, including gods and demons, are Semitic, not European. So it is Yeshua the Mashiah, not Jesus the Christ. One may recognize that Saint James is not from London or China but a Jew from Jerusalem, and that it would be best to call him Yakobos as in biblical Greek, or better, Yaakov, reflecting his name in Aramaic and Hebrew. Similar convictions about reflecting original language and place have led me to a spelling I have presented, with variations, in rendering Greek lyric poetry and the philosophers Herakleitos and Plotinos.

The main lesson from all this is that whatever one does will make a lot of people furious. One cannot be consistent, and therefore one is an incompetent and worse. Any linguistic change troubles like new currency and stamps. Even God and his envoy Adam had trouble in naming and spelling in the Garden. In these often pained choices I have been helped hugely by my former colleague at Wesleyan University, William McCulloh, with whom I collaborated for both *Greek Lyric Poetry* (1961) and *Sappho: Lyrics in the Original Greek and Translations* (1965). Now, as in the past, it is his scholarship against my amateurism. I learn from him. McCulloh is absolute in making me note all sins. So what you find here may be enervating but not slipshod. Not on McCulloh's watch, for which I am endlessly grateful.

After apologies, here are a few examples.

In the English translation of Sappho's poems, I tend to use the Greek *k* rather than the Latin *c*, *f* rather than *ph*, and I follow the vowels as we read them in Greek. So Sappho in the poems is *Psapfo*, which is how she calls herself in Aiolic Greek, the dialect of Lesbos. For all other names in Aiolic, I stick to standard Attic. Her *Afrodita* is *Afroditi*. Sappho's island compatriot poet Alkaios, who is traditionally Latinized as *Alcaeus*, remains *Alkaios* as Greeks and Germans render his name. Other than *Sappho*, when the name is so well recognized in English that change may confuse or offend, I stick to the familiar spelling. So for instance, I keep *Helen* and *Socrates*, and do not suggest *Elena* and *Sokratis*.* But for years I have found it painful to keep the final Latin *us* for Greek *os*,

---

* I leave the hardest part of this essay to a footnote, still pondering on *phi* and *eta*, whether Greek φ = English *ph* or *f*, and whether Greek η = English *e* or *i*, and a few other enigma. My reasonable premise is that a literary translation is not a chart for imitating ancient phonemes. While it is fun to have an approximate knowledge of ancient Greek phonology, such knowledge is marginal in our pact with the original poet to be a poet in English faithful to song.

McCulloh correctly notes that φ in ancient Greek was not a voiceless bilabial fricative *f* but an aspirated plosive *p*, like the *p* in *pot*.

Our traditional preference for the Latin *ph* misleads us as a good emissary and so it is *Plotinos,* not *Plotinus,* and the Cycladic island is *Serifos,* not *Seriphus* as on old English maps.

In general I prefer to be closer to what Italians do with *Cicero* and Greeks with *Euripides.* They pronounce all common words and ancient names as they do Italian and modern Greek and do not aspirate their φ. Hence, Greeks sitting in an ancient amphitheater or standing in an Orthodox church understand the old

---

for a Greek utterance. Roman Latin construed the double consonant *ph* to represent the Greek aspirated *p.* It worked until approximately the fourth century B.C.E., when the aspirated Greek *p* evolved into a fricative *f.* In Latin the *ph* evolved into fricative *f,* which is how it remains today. In English the initial *ph* reveals only that etymologically the word came to us through Latin from Greek, a nice trophy, but offering just *f.* No more.

How can we hear an ancient Greek voice, since for most of us Latin *ph* fails? No way. English is not Greek. In modern tongues and by international phonetic convention, φ (*phi*) is not a plosive *p* but the voiceless bilabial fricative *f.* Hence, when the English name is not too sacred to change, I like to render φ as *f* rather than Latin *ph,* keeping us close to Greek and escaping a Latin presence.

Ph is a powerful Latin hangover, not a Greek smile, and the Romanization of gods and names still invades Greece. Similarly, it is hard in Europe and the West to forget our practice of Hellenizing and Anglicizing Aramaic and Hebrew biblical names and hence we still have *Israelite* for *Yisraeli,* and *Elizabeth* for *Elisheva.* The forces of Latin grammar and spelling remain in Saxon English, and until recently good scholars wrote both introduction and annotation to Greek texts in Latin as did Lobel and Page and Eva-Maria Voigt in their essential volumes of Sappho's Greek fragments.

To be loyal to an ancient aspirated *phi* we should write *pilosopy.* Then, the initial *p* would be a plosive *p* and a bit closer to the classical and archaic φ. No one offers that nutty solution. Latin tongues don't bother. Spanish gives us *filosofía.* Why are we loyal to a sign that no longer signifies an original sound in Greek? The strong tradition of shuffling Greek words through an adoptive Latin gives us *Alcaeus,* not *Alkaios,* for Sappho's contemporary poet friend in Lesbos. I find the preponderance and authority of Latinization tough to swallow. As Greece becomes a vivid entity, it is easy to switch to Alkaios. *Plato* remains *Plato,* not *Platon,* the "broad-shouldered." And when writing about Sappho, it is *Sappho.* But in her poems, she is *Psapfo* and, for all the reasons given above, not the mixed signal of *Psappho.*

chanted Greek. Whatever script is used to record Sappho in another tongue, as she sings in Greek she must sing in English. The smallest of her surviving Greek fragments echoes with music.

If you hear some here, you may forgive the graphic signs.

W.B.
October 2005

AFRODITI OF
THE FLOWERS
AT KNOSSOS

Ποικιλόθρον᾽ ἀθανάτ᾽ Ἀφρόδιτα,
παῖ Δίος δολόπλοκε, λίσσομαί σε,
μή μ᾽ ἄσαισι μηδ᾽ ὀνίαισι δάμνα,
πότνια, θῦμον,

ἀλλὰ τυίδ᾽ ἔλθ᾽, αἴ ποτα κἀτέρωτα
τὰς ἔμας αὔδας ἀίοισα πήλοι
ἔκλυες, πάτρος δὲ δόμον λίποισα
χρύσιον ἦλθες

ἄρμ᾽ ὑπασδεύξαισα· κάλοι δέ σ᾽ ἆγον
ὤκεες στροῦθοι περὶ γᾶς μελαίνας
πύκνα δίννεντες πτέρ᾽ ἀπ᾽ ὠράνωἴθε-
ρος διὰ μέσσω,

αἶψα δ᾽ ἐξίκοντο· σὺ δ᾽, ὦ μάκαιρα,
μειδιαίσαισ᾽ ἀθανάτωι προσώπωι
ἤρε᾽ ὄττι δηὖτε πέπονθα κὤττι
δηὖτε κάλημμι

κὤττι μοι μάλιστα θέλω γένεσθαι
μαινόλαι θύμωι· τίνα δηὖτε πείθω
ἄψ σ᾽ ἄγην ἐς ϝὰν φιλότατα; τίς σ᾽, ὦ
Ψάπφ᾽, ἀδικήει;

καὶ γὰρ αἰ φεύγει, ταχέως διώξει,
αἰ δὲ δῶρα μὴ δέκετ᾽, ἀλλὰ δώσει,
αἰ δὲ μὴ φίλει, ταχέως φιλήσει
κωὐκ ἐθέλοισα.

Prayer to Afroditi

On your dappled throne eternal Afroditi,
cunning daughter of Zeus,
I beg you, do not crush my heart
    with pain, O lady,

but come here if ever before
you heard my voice from far away,
and yielding left your father's house
    of gold and came,

yoking birds to your chariot. Beautiful
quick sparrows whirring on beating wings
took you from heaven down to mid sky
    over the black earth

and soon arrived. O blessed one,
on your deathless face a smile,
you asked me what I am suffering
    and why I call you,

what I most want to happen
in my crazy heart. "Whom shall I persuade
again to take you into her love? Who,
    O Psapfo, wrongs you?

If she runs away, soon she will pursue.
If she scorns gifts, now she will bribe.
If she doesn't love, soon she will love
    even unwillingly."

ἔλθε μοι καὶ νῦν, χαλέπαν δὲ λῦσον
ἐκ μερίμναν, ὄσσα δέ μοι τέλεσσαι
θῦμος ἰμέρρει, τέλεσον, σὺ δ᾽ αὔτα
σύμμαχος ἔσσο.

Come to me now and loosen me
from blunt agony. Labor
and fill my heart with fire. Stand by me
        and be my ally.

2

δεῦρύ μ᾽ ἐκ Κρήτας ἐπ[ὶ τόνδ]ε ναῦον
ἄγνον ὄππ[αι τοι] χάριεν μὲν ἄλσος
μαλί[αν], βῶμοι δὲ τεθυμιάμε-
νοι [λι]βανώτωι·

ἐν δ᾽ ὕδωρ ψῦχρον κελάδει δι᾽ ὔσδων
μαλίνων, βρόδοισι δὲ παῖς ὀ χῶρος
ἐσκίαστ᾽, αἰθυσσομένων δὲ φύλλων
κῶμα κατέρρει·

ἐν δὲ λείμων ἰππόβοτος τέθαλεν
ἠρίνοισιν ἄνθεσιν, αἰ δ᾽ ἄηται
μέλλιχα πνέοισιν [
[   ]

ἔνθα δὴ σὺ . . . . ἔλοισα Κύπρι
χρυσίαισιν ἐν κυλίκεσσιν ἄβρως
ὀμμεμείχμενον θαλίαισι νέκταρ
οἰνοχόαισον

6

Afroditi of the Flowers at Knossos

Leave Kriti and come here to this holy
temple with your graceful grove
of apple trees and altars smoking
    with frankincense.

Icy water babbles through apple branches
and roses leave shadow on the ground
and bright shaking leaves pour down
    profound sleep.

Here is a meadow where horses graze
amid wild blossoms of the spring and soft winds
    blow aroma

of honey. Afroditi, take the nectar
and delicately pour it into gold
wine cups and mingle joy with
    our celebration.

154

πλήρης μὲν ἐφαίνετ᾽ ἀ σελάννα
αἰ δ᾽ ὡς περὶ βῶμον ἐστάθησαν

16 INCERT.

Κρῆσσαί νύ ποτ᾽ ὦδ᾽ ἐμμελέως πόδεσσιν
ὤρχηντ᾽ ἀπάλοισ᾽ ἀμφ᾽ ἐρόεντα βῶμον,

πόας τέρεν ἄνθος μάλακον μάτεισαι.

Moon and Women

The moon appeared in her fullness
when women took their place around the altar

Dancers at a Kritan Altar

Kritan women once danced supplely
around a beautiful altar with light feet,

crushing the soft flowers of grass.

20

]επιθεσμα
]ε γάνος δὲ και . [
    ]

    τ]ύχαι σὺν ἔσλαι
λί]μενος κρέτησαι
    γ]ας μελαίνας
]

    ]έλοισι ναῦται
    ] μεγάλαις ἀήται[ς
    ]α κἀπὶ χέρσω
]

    ]μοθεν πλέοι [
    ]δε τὰ φόρτι᾽ εἰκ[
    ]νατιμ᾽ ἐπεὶ κ [
    ]

    ]ρέοντι πόλλαι[
    ]αιδέκα[
    ]ει
    ]

    ]ιν ἔργα
    ] χέρσω [

10

In Time of Storm

Brightness

and with good luck
we will reach the harbor
and black earth

We sailors have no will
in big blasts of wind,
hoping for dry land

and to sail
our cargo
floating about

Many
labors
until dry land

17

Πλάσιον δή μ᾽ [εὐχομέναι φανείη
πότνι᾽ Ἦρα σὰ χ[αρίεσσα μόρφα
τὰν ἀράταν Ἀτ[ρέιδαι   κλῆ-
τοι βασίληες·

ἐκτελέσσαντες μ[άλα πόλλ᾽ ἄεθλα
πρῶτα μὲν πὲρ Ἴ[λιον, ἔν τε πόντωι,
τυίδ᾽ ἀπορμάθεν[τες ὄδον περαίνην
οὐκ ἐδύναντο,

πρὶν σὲ καὶ Δί᾽ ἀντ[ίαον κάλεσσαι
καὶ Θυώνας ἰμε[ρόεντα παῖδα·
νῦν δὲ κ[ἄμοι πραϋμένης ἄρηξον
κὰτ τὸ πάλ[αιον.

ἄγνα καὶ κά[λα
π]αρθ[εν
ἀ]μφι [

ἔμμενα[ι
ἴ]ρ᾽ ἀπίκεσθαι

To Lady Hera

Be near me Lady Hera while I pray
for your graceful form to appear,
to which the sons of Atreus prayed,
those dazzling kings

who did bountiful deeds,
first at Troy, then on the sea,
but sailing the road to this island,
they could not reach it

till they called on you and Zeus god of suppliants,
and Dionysos lovely son of Thyoni.
Now be gentle and help me too
as in old days,

holy and beautiful
virgin
in circles

to sail safely
to the shrine

9

π]αρκαλειοιτασε [
]παν οὐκεχη[
ερ ἐόρταν

]μαν [Ἥ]ραι τελε[
].ωνέμ[
]. ᾶς ἄ. [
]υσαι [

40   INCERT. 13

σοὶ δ᾽ ἔγω λεύκας †επιδωμον† αἴγος

κἀπιλείψω τοι

14

Invitation

Invitation for one
not all
to come to a feast

for Hera   accomplishing
as long
as
I am alive

Sacrifice

To you I will pour wine

over flesh of a white goat

140

κατθναίσκει, Κυθέρη, ἄβρος Ἄδωνις· τί κε θεῖμεν;
καττύπτεσθε, κόραι, καὶ κατερείκεσθε κίθωνας.

168

ὦ τὸν Ἄδωνιν

Death of Adonis

Afroditi, delicate Adonis is dying.
                      What should we do?

Virgins, beat your breasts
                      and tear your garments.

Adonis Gone

O for Adonis!

33

αἴθ᾽ ἔγω, χρυσοστέφαν᾽ Ἀφρόδιτα,
τόνδε τὸν πάλον λαχοίην

87e, f

β]ασιλη

]ν᾽ σοι
]
]εσιππ[

To Afroditi

O gold-crowned Afroditi,
if only I could win this lot!

Afroditi

Queen
to you
a horse

159

σύ τε κἄμος θεράπων Ἔρος

86

].ακάλα.[
αἰγιόχω λα[
]. Κυθέρη' εὔχομ[
]ον ἔχοισα θῦμο[ν
κλ]ῦθί μ' ἄρας αἴ π[οτα κἀτέρωτα
]ας προλίποισα κ[
]. πεδ' ἔμαν ἰώ[
]ν χαλέπαι.[

Afroditi to Psapfo

Both you Psapfo and my servant Eros

Days of Harshness

Quiet
Zeus
of the goatskin shield

and Kythereia
I pray

holding a good heart,
and if ever

like other days when you left Kypros,
hear my prayer

and come
to my
severities

44a

Φοίβωι χρυσοκό]μαι τὸν ἔτικτε Κόω κ[όρα
μίγεισ᾽ ὐψινέφει [Κρ]ονίδαι μεγαλωνύμωι·
Ἄρτεμις δὲ θέων] μέγαν ὄρκον ἀπώμοσε·
νὴ τὰν σὰν κεφάλ]αν ἄϊ πάρθενος ἔσσομαι
ἄδμης οἰοπό]λων ὀρέων κορύφαισ᾽ ἔπι
θηρεύοισ᾽· ἄγι καὶ τά]δε νεῦσον ἔμαν χάριν·
ὢς εἶπ᾽· αὐτὰρ ἔνευ]σε θέων μακάρων πάτηρ·
πάρθενον δ᾽ ἐλαφάβ]ολον ἀγροτέραν θέοι
ἄνθρωποί τε κάλε]ισιν ἐπωνύμιον μέγα·
κήναι λυσιμέλης] Ἔρος οὐδάμα πίλναται,

84

]τονόνε. [. ?] . οσε[
]άβροις ἐπιχ[?]ημ[
]αν Ἀρτεμι[

Artemis on Solitary Mountains

Gold-haired Phoebus borne by Koios's daughter
after she joined with Kronos's son Zeus god of high clouds
    and high name.
Artemis swore the great oath of the gods to Zeus:
"By your head, I shall always be a virgin
untamed, hunting on peaks of solitary mountains.
Come, grant me this grace!"
So she spoke. Then the father of the blessed gods
nodded his consent. Now gods and mortals
call her by her thrilling eponym, *The Virgin Deer Hunter.*
Eros, loosener of limbs, never comes near her

Artemis

blame
delicate
Artemis

NIGHTINGALE

104a

Ἔσπερε πάντα φέρων ὄσα φαίνολις ἐσκέδασ᾽ Αὔως,
†φέρεις ὄιν, φέρεις αἶγα,† φέρεις ἄπυ μάτερι παῖδα.

104b

ἀστέρων πάντων ὁ κάλλιστος

Evening Star

Hesperos, you bring home all the bright dawn
scattered,
bring home the sheep,
bring home the goat, bring the child home
to her mother.

Hesperos

Of all stars the most beautiful

34

ἄστερες μὲν ἀμφὶ κάλαν σελάνναν
ἂψ ἀπυκρύπτοισι φάεννον εἶδος,
ὄπποτα πλήθοισα μάλιστα λάμπηι
   γᾶν

ἀργυρία

168c

            ποικίλλεται μὲν
γαῖα πολυστέφανος

Moon

Stars around the beautiful moon
conceal their luminous form
when in her fullness she shines
    on the earth

in silver

Earth

Earth is embroidered
with rainbow-colored garlands

136

ἦρος ἄγγελος ἱμερόφωνος ἀήδων

101a

ἄχει δ'ἐκ πετάλων ἄδεα τέττιξ, πτερύγων δ' ὔπα
κακχέει λιγύραν <πύκνον> ἀοίδαν, <θέρος> ὄπποτα
φλόγιον †καθέταν ἐπιπτάμενον καταυδείη†

Nightingale

Nightingale with your lovely voice
you are the herald of spring

Cicada

Flaming summer
charms the earth with its own fluting,
and under leaves
the cicada scrapes its tiny wings together
and incessantly
pours out full shrill song

42

ταῖσι <δὲ> ψῦχρος μὲν ἔγεντ᾽ ὀ θῦμος
πὰρ δ᾽ ἴεισι τὰ πτέρα

178

Γέλλως παιδοφιλωτέρα

Doves Playing Dead

When their souls grew cold they dropped
their wings to their sides

*Of Gello Who Died Young, Whose Ghost
Haunts Little Children*

She was even fonder
of children than Gello.

52

ψαύην δ᾽ οὐ δοκίμωμ᾽ ὀράνω †δυσπαχέα†

157

πότνια Αὔως

123

ἀρτίως μὲν ἀ χρυσοπέδιλος Αὔως

World

I could not hope
to touch the sky
with my two arms

Eos

Lady Dawn

Dawn

Suddenly
Dawn in gold sandals

WALKING TO A
WEDDING

98a

..]θος· ὰ γάρ με γέννα[τ

σ]φᾶς ἐπ᾽ ἀλικίας μεγ[αν
κ]όσμον, αἴ τις ἔχηι φόβα<ι>ς[
πορφύρωι κατελιξαμένα πλόκωι,

ἔμμεναι μάλα τοῦτο δ[ή·
ἀλλ᾽ ὰ ξανθοτέραις ἔχη[
ταὶς κόμαις δάιδος προ[

σ]τεφάνοισιν ἐπαρτία[ις
ἀνθέων ἐριθαλέων·
μ]ιτράναν δ᾽ ἀρτίως κλ[

ποικίλαν ἀπὺ Σαρδίω[ν
. . .]. αονίας πόλις [

38

Hair Yellower Than Torch Flame

My mother used to say

in her youth
it was a great ornament to wear
a purple ribbon

looped in her hair. But a girl
with hair yellower than torch flame
need wear just

a wreath of blooming
flowers, or lately maybe
a colorful headband

from Sardis
or some Ionian city

24a, b, c

(a)   ]ανάγα[
              ]εμνάσεσθ᾽ ἀ[
     κ]αὶ γὰρ ἄμμες ἐν νεό[τατι
     ταῦτ᾽ [ἐ]πόημμεν·

     πόλλα [μ]ὲν γὰρ καὶ κά[λα
     ...η . [ ]μεν, πόλι[
     ἀ]μμε[.]ὀ[ξ]είαις δ[

(b) ζ]ωρμ[εν .
     ]εναντ[
     [τ]όλμαν[
     ]ανθρω[

(c) .εδαφ[
     [λ]επτοφών[

40

Time of Youth

You will
remember
we did these things
in our youth,

many and beautiful things.

In the city
for us the harsh

We live
opposite

a daring
person

stone foundation
thin-voiced

125

†ταυταόρα† ἐστεφαναπλόκην

132

Ἔστι μοι κάλα πάις χρυσίοισιν ἀνθέμοισιν
ἐμφέρη<ν> ἔχοισα μόρφαν Κλέις ἀγαπάτα,
ἀντὶ τᾶς ἔγωὐδὲ Λυδίαν παῖσαν οὐδ᾽ ἐράνναν . . .

Of a Young Lover

When I was young I wove garlands

My Daughter

I have a beautiful child like a gold flower
in form. I wouldn't trade
my darling Kleis for all Lydia or lovely . . .

122

ἄνθε᾽ ἀμέργοισαν παῖδ᾽ ἄγαν ἀπάλαν

105a, c

(a) οἶον τὸ γλυκύμαλον ἐρεύθεται ἄκρωι ἐπ᾽ ὔσδωι,
ἄκρον ἐπ᾽ ἀκροτάτωι, λελάθοντο δὲ μαλοδρόπηες·
οὐ μὰν ἐκλελάθοντ᾽, ἀλλ᾽ οὐκ ἐδύναντ᾽ ἐπίκεσθαι.

(c) οἴαν τὰν ὐάκινθον ἐν ὤρεσι ποίμενες ἄνδρες
πόσσι καταστείβοισι, χάμαι δέ τε πόρφυρον ἄνθος

Wildflowers

A tender girl picking wildflowers

The Virgin

Like a sweet apple reddening on a high branch,
on the tip of the topmost branch and forgotten
by the apple pickers—no, beyond their reach.

Like a hyacinth in the mountains that shepherd men
trample down with their feet, and on the earth
the purple flower

153

πάρθενον ἀδύφωνον

107

ἦρ' ἔτι παρθενίας ἐπιβάλλομαι;

114

παρθενία, παρθενία, ποῖ με λίποισ' ἀποίχηι;
†οὐκέτι ἥξω πρὸς σέ, οὐκέτι ἥξω†

Girl

A sweet-voiced girl

Remorse

Do I still long for my virginity?

Words with Virginity

Virginity, virginity, where have you gone, leaving me
    abandoned?
No longer will I come to you. No longer will I come.

103

] . εν τὸ γὰρ ἐννεπε[.]η προβ[
] . ατε τὰν εὔποδα νύμφαν [
]τα παῖδα Κρονίδα τὰν ἰόκ[ολπ]ον [
].ς ὄργαν θεμένα τὰν ἰόκ[ολ]πος α[
] . . . ἄγναι Χάριτες Πιέριδέ[ς τε] Μοῖ[σαι
] . [. ὄ]πποτ᾿ ἀοιδαι φρέν[. . .]αν . [
]σαιοισα λιγύραν [ἀοί]δαν
γά]μβρον, ἄσαροι γὰρ ὐμαλικ[
]σε φόβαισι θεμένα λύρα . [
] . . . η χρυσοπέδιλ<λ> [ο]ς Αὔως [

48

The Lyre Speaks

Tell of the bride with beautiful feet
let Artemis

the violet-robed daughter of Zeus
let the violet-robed put aside her anger.

Come holy Graces and Pierian Muses
when songs are in the heart
listening to a clear song

The bridegroom   annoying   companions

her hair   placing the lyre

Dawn with gold sandals

44

Κυπρο.[   ]ας·
κάρυξ ἦλθε θε[   ]ελε[. . .] . θεις
Ἴδαος ταδεκα . . . φ[. .] . ις τάχυς ἄγγελος

τάς τ᾽ ἄλλας Ἀσίας . [.]δε . αν κλέος ἄφθιτον·
Ἕκτωρ καὶ συνέταιρ[ο]ι ἄγοισ᾽ ἐλικώπιδα
Θήβας ἐξ ἰέρας Πλακίας τ᾽ ἀ [π᾽ ἀι]ν <ν>άω
ἄβραν Ἀνδρομάχαν ἐνὶ ναῦσιν ἐπ᾽ ἄλμυρον
πόντον· πόλλα δ᾽ [ἐλί]γματα χρύσια κἄμματα
πορφύρ[α] καταΰτ[με]να, ποίκιλ᾽ ἀθύρματα,
ἀργύρα τ᾽ ἀνάριθμα ποτήρια κἀλέφαις.

ὢς εἶπ᾽· ὀτραλέως δ᾽ ἀνόρουσε πάτ[η]ρ φίλος·
φάμα δ᾽ ἦλθε κατὰ πτόλιν εὐρύχορον φίλοις.
αὔτικ᾽ Ἰλίαδαι σατίναι[ς] ὐπ᾽ ἐυτρόχοις
ἄγον αἰμιόνοις, ἐπ[έ]βαινε δὲ παῖς ὄχλος
γυναίκων τ᾽ ἄμα παρθενίκα[ν] τ . [. .] οσφύρων,
χῶρις δ᾽ αὖ Περάμοιο θύγ[α]τρες[
ἴππ[οις] δ᾽ ἄνδρες ὔπαγον ὐπ᾽ ἀρ[ματ-
π[   ]ες ἠίθεοι, μεγάλω[σ]τι δ[
δ[   ] . ἀνίοχοι φ[. . . . .] . [
π[᾽]α.ο[

          ἴ]κελοι θέοι[ς
          ] ἄγνον ἀολ[λε-
ὄρμαται[   ]νον ἐς Ἴλιο[ν,
αὖλος δ᾽ ἀδυ[μ]έλης [κίθαρίς] τ᾽ ὀνεμίγνυ[το
καὶ ψ[ό]φο[ς κ]ροτάλ[ων, λιγέ]ως δ᾽ ἄρα πάρ[θενοι

Wedding of Andromache and Hektor

From Kypros
a herald came
Idaos the swift-running Trojan messenger

telling of the wedding's imperishable fame in all Asia:
"Hektor and his companions are bringing dancing-eyed
delicate Andromache on ships over the salt sea
from holy Thibai and Plakia's flowing waters
along with many gold bracelets and purple
fragrant clothes, exquisite adornments
and countless silver cups and ivory."

He spoke, and Hektor's dear father sprang to his feet
and news spread to friends throughout the spacious city.
Instantly the sons of Ilos, founder of Troy,
yoked mules to carriages with smooth-running wheels,
and a whole crowd of women and slender-ankled virgins
        climbed aboard.
The daughters of Priamos came in their own carts,
and young unmarried men yoked stallions to chariots.
In great spirit
charioteers

                        moved like gods
                        holy all together
and set out   for Ilion
in a confusion of sweet-voiced flutes and kithara
and small crashing castanets,

ἄειδον μέλος ἄγν[ον ἴκα]νε δ᾽ ἐς αἴθ[ερα
ἄχω θεσπεσία γελ[
πάνται δ᾽ ἦς κὰτ ὄδο[ις
κράτηρες φίαλαί τ᾽ ὀ[. . .]υεδε[. .]. .εακ[.]. [
μύρρα καὶ κασία λίβανός τ᾽ ὀνεμείχνυτο

γύναικες δ᾽ ἐλέλυσδον ὄσαι προγενέστερα[ι,
πάντες δ᾽ ἄνδρες ἐπήρατον ἴαχον ὄρθιον
Πάον᾽ ὀνκαλέοντες ἐκάβολον εὐλύραν,
ὔμνην δ᾽ Ἔκτορα κ᾽Ανδρομάχαν θεοεικέλο[ις.

and young virgins sang a loud heavenly song
whose amazing echo pierced the ether of the sky.
Everywhere in the streets
were bowls and cups.
Myrrh and cassia and frankincense rode on the wind.

Old women shouted in happiness
and all the men sang out with thrilling force,
calling on far-shooting Paean Apollo nimble on the lyre
and sang to godlike Hektor and Andromache.

27

] καὶ γὰρ δὴ σὺ πάις ποτ[

. . .]ιϟης μέλπεσθ᾽ ἄγι ταῦτα[

. .] ζάλεξαι, κἄμμ᾽ ἀπὺ τωδεκ[
   ἄ]δρα χάρισσαι·

σ]τείχομεν γὰρ ἐς γάμον· εὖ δε[
   κα]ὶ σὺ τοῦτ᾽, ἀλλ᾽ ὄττι τάχιστα[
   πα]ρ[θ]ένοις ἄπ[π]εμπε, θέοι[
      ]εν ἔχοιεν

      ] ὄδος μ[έ]γαν εἰς Ὄλ[υμπον
   ἀ]νθρω[π   ]αίκ. [

54

Walking to a Wedding

Yes you were once a child
come sing these things
talk to us and give us
      your grace

We are walking to a wedding, and surely
you know too, but quickly as you can
send the young virgins away. May gods
      have

Yet for men   road to
      great Olympos

115

Τίωι σ᾽, ὦ φίλε γάμβρε, κάλως ἐικάσδω;
ὄρπακι βραδίνωι σε μάλιστ᾽ ἐικάσδω.

113

οὐ γὰρ †ἐτέρα νῦν† πάις ὦ γάμβρε τεαύτα

108

ὦ κάλα, ὦ χαρίεσσα κόρα

Song to the Groom

What are you like, lovely bridegroom?
You are most like a slender sapling.

Song for the Bride

O bridegroom, there is no other woman now
    like her

Lesbian Bride

O beautiful, O graceful girl

161

τανδεφυλασσετε ἐννε[..]οι γάμβροι [.....]υ
πολίων βασίληες

103b

]ϱηον θαλάμω τοδεσ[
]ις εὔποδα νύμφαν ἀβ
] . νυνδ[
]ν μοι·[
]ας γε.[

Guarding the Bride

Take care of her
O bridegrooms
O kings of cities!

Chamber

Room
the bride with her beautiful feet
now
for me

141a, b

(a) κῆ δ᾽ ἀμβροσίας μὲν
κράτηρ ἐκέκρατ᾽
Ἔρμαις δ᾽ ἔλων ὄλπιν θέοισ᾽ ἐοινοχόησε.

(b) κῆνοι δ᾽ ἄρα πάντες
καρχάσι᾽ ἦχον
κἄλειβον ἀράσαντο δὲ πάμπαν ἔσλα
γάμβρωι.

Hermis at a Wedding

There a bowl of ambrosia
was mixed, and Hermis
took the jug and poured wine for the gods
and then they all
held out cups and poured
libations and prayed for all blessings
for the groom.

103C a, b

]φερην[

Ἀρ]χεάνασσ[

]δήποτ᾽ ὀνα[

]εν ἐπηρατ[

ἔ]κλυον ε[

Κ]ραννίαδες δ[

πα]ρθενικαις.[

Fragments

Carry

Arheanassa

once

in lovely

heard

virgins

of the springs

III

ἴψοι δὴ τὸ μέλαθρον·
ὑμήναον·
ἀέρρετε τέκτονες ἄνδρες·
ὑμήναον.
γάμβρος (εἰσ)έρχεται ἴσος Ἄρευι,
<ὑμήναον. >
ἄνδρος μεγάλω πόλυ μέσδων.
<ὑμήναον. >

112

Ὄλβιε γάμβρε, σοὶ μὲν δὴ γάμος ὡς ἄραο
ἐκτετέλεστ᾽, ἔχῃς δὲ πάρθενον ἂν ἄραο . . .
σοὶ χάριεν μὲν εἶδος, ὄππατα δ᾽ . . .
μέλλιχ᾽, ἔρος δ᾽ ἐπ᾽ ἰμέρτωι κέχυται προσώπωι
. . . τετίμακ᾽ ἔξοχά σ᾽ Ἀφροδίτα

To Hymen, Wedding God

High! Raise the roof!
O Hymen.
Lift it up, carpenters!
O Hymen.
The bridegroom is coming, the equal of Aris,
O Hymen.
taller than a giant!
O Hymen!

Song to Groom and Bride

Happy groom, your marriage you prayed for
has happened. You have the virgin bride
of your prayer.

You the bride are a form of grace,
your eyes honey.
Desire rains on your exquisite face.

Afroditi has honored you exceedingly

30

νύκτ[.

πάρθενοι δ[
παννυχίσδοι[σ]αι [
σὰν ἀείδοιεν φ[ιλότατα καὶ νύμ-
φας ἰοκόλπω.

ἀλλ᾽ ἐγέρθεις, ἠϊθ[έοις
στεῖχε σοὶς ὐμάλικ[ας, ὠς ἐλάσσω
ἤπερ ὄσσον ἀ λιγύφω[νος ὄρνις
ὔπνον [ἴ]δωμεν.

Night Song

Night

Virgins
will all night long sing
of the love between you and your bride
in her violet robe.

Wake and call out young men
of your age,
and tonight we shall sleep less than
the bright-voiced nightingale

110

Θυρώρωι πόδες ἐπτορόγυιοι,
τὰ δὲ σάμβαλα πεμπεβόηα,
πίσσυγγοι δὲ δέκ᾽ ἐξεπόναισαν.

43   (lines 3–9)

            ] [[κ]]αλος
            ] ἄκαλα κλόνει
            ] κάματος φρένα
            ]ε κατισδάνε[ι]
            ] ἀλλ᾽ ἄγιτ᾽, ὦ φίλαι,
            ], ἄγχι γὰρ ἀμέρα.

68

A Guard outside the Bridal Chamber Who Keeps the Bride's Friends from Rescuing Her

The doorkeeper's feet are seven fathoms long.
It took five oxhides for his sandals
and ten shoemakers to cobble them together.

End of a Party

Beautiful
he throws peace into frenzy
and exhaustion and dumbs the mind.
Sitting

But come, my friends.
Soon daybreak.

YOU BURN US

31

Φαίνεταί μοι κῆνος ἴσος θέοισιν
ἔμμεν᾽ ὤνηρ, ὄττις ἐνάντιός τοι
ἰσδάνει καὶ πλάσιον ἆδυ φωνεί-
σας ὐπακούει

καὶ γελαίσας ἰμέροεν, τό μ᾽ ἦ μὰν
καρδίαν ἐν στήθεσιν ἐπτόαισεν,
ὠς γὰρ ἔς σ᾽ ἴδω βρόχε᾽ ὤς με φώναι-
σ᾽ οὐδ᾽ ἒν ἔτ᾽ εἴκει,

ἀλλ᾽ ἄκαν μὲν γλῶσσά <μ᾽> ἔαγε λέπτον
δ᾽ αὔτικα χρῶι πῦρ ὐπαδεδρόμηκεν,
ὀππάτεσσι δ᾽ οὐδ᾽ ἒν ὄρημμ᾽, ἐπιρρόμ-
βεισι δ᾽ ἄκουαι,

κὰδ δέ μ᾽ ἴδρως κακχέεται τρόμος δὲ
παῖσαν ἄγρει, χλωροτέρα δὲ ποίας
ἔμμι, τεθνάκην δ᾽ ὀλίγω 'πιδεύης
φαίνομ᾽ ἔμ᾽ αὔται·

ἀλλὰ πὰν τόλματον, ἐπεὶ †καὶ πένητα†

72

Seizure

To me he seems equal to gods,
the man who sits facing you
and hears you near as you speak
    softly and laugh

in a sweet echo that jolts
the heart in my ribs. Now
when I look at you a moment
    my voice is empty

and can say nothing as my tongue
cracks and slender fire races
under my skin. My eyes are dead
    to light, my ears

pound, and sweat pours over me.
I convulse, greener than grass
and feel my mind slip as I go
    close to death.

Yet I must suffer, even poor

168b

Δέδυκε μὲν ἀ σελάννα
καὶ Πληΐαδες· μέσαι δὲ
νύκτες, παρὰ δ᾽ ἔρχετ᾽ ὤρα
ἔγω δὲ μόνα κατεύδω.

91

ἀσαροτέρας οὐδάμα πΩϊρανα σέθεν τύχοισαν

Alone

The moon has set and
the Pleiades. Middle
of the night, time spins
away and I lie alone.

Emptiness

Never have I found you more repulsive,
O Irana.

47

Ἔρος δ᾽ ἐτίναξέ μοι
φρένας, ὡς ἄνεμος κὰτ ὄρος δρύσιν ἐμπέτων.

54

ἔλθοντ᾽ ἐξ ὀράνω πορφυρίαν περθέμενον χλάμυν

Eros

Love shook my heart like wind
on a mountain punishing oak trees.

Love

Eros came out of heaven,
dressed in a purple cape

16

Ο]ἰ μὲν ἰππήων στρότον οἰ δὲ πέσδων
οἰ δὲ νάων φαῖσ᾽ ἐπ[ὶ] γᾶν μέλαι[ν]αν
ἔ]μμεναι κάλλιστον, ἔγω δὲ κῆν᾽ ὄτ-
τω τις ἔραται·

πά]γχυ δ᾽ εὔμαρες σύνετον πόησαι
π]άντι τ[ο]ῦτ᾽, ἀ γὰρ πόλυ περσκέθοισα
κάλλος [ἀνθ]ρώπων Ἐλένα [τὸ]ν ἄνδρα
τὸν [πανάρ]ιστον

καλλ[ίποι]σ᾽ ἔβα ᾽ς Τροΐαν πλέοι[σα
κωὐδ[ὲ πα]ῖδος οὐδὲ φίλων το[κ]ήων
πά[μπαν] ἐμνάσθη, ἀλλὰ παράγαγ᾽ αὔταν
]σαν

]αμπτον γὰρ [
] . . . κούφως τ[   ]οησ.[.]ν
. .]με. νῦν Ἀνακτορί[ας ὀ]νέμναι-
σ᾽ οὐ] παρεοίσας,

τᾶ]ς κε βολλοίμαν ἔρατόν τε βᾶμα
κἀμάρυχμα λάμπρον ἴδην προσώπω
ἢ τὰ Λύδων ἄρματα κἀν ὄπλοισι
πεσδομ]άχεντας.

] . μεν οὐ δύνατον γένεσθαι
] . ν ἀνθρωπ[. . . π]εδέχην δ᾽ ἄρασθαι
]

τ᾽ ἐξ ἀδοκή[τω.

78

Supreme Sight on the Black Earth

Some say cavalry and others claim
infantry or a fleet of long oars
is the supreme sight on the black earth.
      I say it is

the one you love. And easily proved.
Didn't Helen, who far surpassed
all in beauty, desert the best of men
      her husband and king

and sail off to Troy and forget
her daughter and dear parents? Merely
love's gaze made her bend
      and led her

from her path.
These tales
remind me now of Anaktoria
      who is gone.

And I would rather see her supple step
and motion of light on her face
than chariots of the Lydians or ranks
      of foot soldiers in bronze.

Now this is impossible
yet among the living I pray for a share

unexpectedly.

38

ὄπταις ἄμμε

36

καὶ ποθήω καὶ μάομαι

To Eros

You burn us

Absence

I long and yearn for

74a (lines 2, 4), 74b (line 2), 74c (line 2)

]αιπόλ[   ]ποθο   ]ας ἴδρω
]
] βροδο

51

οὐκ οἶδ᾽ ὄττι θέω· δίχα μοι τὰ νοήμματα

46

                                    ἔγω δ᾽ ἐπὶ μολθάκαν
τύλαν κασπολέω †μέλεα· κἂν μὲν τε τύλαγκας
      ἀσπόλεα†

Goatherd

Goatherd
a rose

longing

sweat

Shall I?

I don't know what to do.
I think yes—and then no.

Pleasure

On a soft pillow
I will lay down my limbs

60

]τύχοισα
]θέλ᾽ †ὠνταπαίσαν
τέ]λεσον νόημμα
]έτων κάλημμι
] πεδὰ θῦμον αἶψα
ὄ]σσα τύχην θελήσῃ[ς
]ϱ ἔμοι μάχεσθα[ι
χ]λιδάναι πίθεισα[ν
]ι, σὺ δ᾽ εὖ γὰϱ οἶσθα

48

ἦλθες, ἔγω δέ σ᾽ ἐμαιόμαν,
ὂν δ᾽ ἔψυξας ἔμαν φρένα καιομέναν πόθωι.

84

Encounter

Finding something
desires
Carry out a plan
suddenly
I call out from my heart.
for all you want to win
fight for me
persuaded by a voluptuous woman
as you know very well

Homecoming

You came and I went mad about you.
You cooled my mind burning with longing.

78

].οναυ[
]ην οὐδε[
]ης ἵμερ[
] αι δ᾿ ἄμα[
] ανθος·[
]μερον[
]ετερπ[

67a

..]ων μα.[

κ]αὶ τοῦτ᾿ ἐπικε . [
δ]αίμων ὀλοφ. [

οὐ μὰν ἐφίλησ.[
νῦν δ᾿ ἔννεκα[

τὸ δ᾿ αἴτιον οὐτ[
οὐδὲν πόλυ[.] . [

Desire

Nor
desire
but together
a flower
desire
I was happy

A God

And this
disastrous
god

I swear did not love
but now because

and the cause neither
nothing much

68a

]ι γάρ μ' ἀπὺ τὰς ἐ . [
      ὔ]μως δ' ἔγεν[το
      ] ἴσαν θέοισιν
     ]ασαν ἀλίτρα[
   Ἀν]δρομέδαν[.] . αξ[
]αρ[. . . .] . α μάκα[ιρ]α
]εον δὲ τρόπον α[.] . ύνη[
   ] κόρον οὐ κατισχε . [
]κα[. . . . .] . Τυνδαρίδαι[ς
]ασυ[.] . . .κα[.] χαρίεντ' ἀ . [
]κ' ἄδολον [μ]ηκέτι συν[
] Μεγάρα . [. .]να[. . .]α[

88

Absent

Away
from her

yet she became
like gods

sinful Andromeda
a blessed one

didn't hold back
her insolence

sons of Tyndareus
gracious

no longer innocent
Megara

146

μήτε μοι μέλι μήτε μέλισσα

76

]αν̣ πα[
]λέ]σειε κ[
]ίη λελα[
]ε θέλω[
]εχην[
]η̣ · ἔφα [
]αλίκ[

45

ἆς θέλετ᾽ ὔμμες

Of Those Unwilling to Take the Bitter
with the Sweet

I care for neither honey
nor the honeybee

Endure

Bring about?

I want
to hang on
she said

I Shall

As long as you want to

RETURN, GONGYLA

94

τεθνάκην δ᾽ ἀδόλως θέλω·
ἄ με ψισδομένα κατελίμπανεν

πόλλα καὶ τόδ᾽ ἔειπέ [μοι·
'ὤιμ᾽ ὡς δεῖνα πεπ[όνθ]αμεν,
Ψάπφ᾽, ἦ μάν σ᾽ ἀέκοισ᾽ ἀπυλιμπάνω.'

τὰν δ᾽ ἔγω τάδ᾽ ἀμειβόμαν·
'χαίροισ᾽ ἔρχεο κἄμεθεν
μέμναισ᾽, οἶσθα γὰρ ὥς σε πεδήπομεν·

αἰ δὲ μή, ἀλλά σ᾽ ἔγω θέλω
ὄμναισαι[....].[.].. αι
.. [   ] καὶ κάλ᾽ ἐπάσχομεν.

πό[λλοις γὰρ στεφάν]οις ἴων
καὶ βρ[όδων κρο]κίων τ᾽ ὔμοι
κα.. [   ] πὰρ ἔμοι περεθήκαο

καὶ πό[λλαις ὑπα]θύμιδας
πλέκ[ταις ἀμφ᾽ ἀ]πάλαι δέραι
ἀνθέων ἔ.[βαλες] πεποημμέναις

καὶ πολλωι[   ]. μύρωι
βρενθείωι.[   ]ρυ[..]ν
ἐξαλείψαο κα[ὶ βασ]ιληίωι

94

To a Friend Gone, Remember

Honestly I wish I were dead.
When she left me she wept

profusely and told me,
"Oh how we've suffered in all this.
Psapfo, I swear I go unwillingly."

And I answered her,
"Be happy, go and remember me,
you know how we worshiped you.

But if not, I want
to remind you
of beautiful days we shared,

how you took wreaths of violets,
roses and crocuses,
and at my side

tied them in garlands
made of flowers
round your tender throat,

and with sweet myrrh oil
worthy of a queen
you anointed your limbs

καὶ στρώμν[αν ἐ]πὶ μολθάκαν
ἀπάλαν πα . [   ] . . . ων
ἐξίης πόθ ο [ν   ] . νίδων

κωὖτε τις[οὔ]τε τι
ἶρον οὐδυ[   ]
ἔπλετ᾽ ὄππ[οθεν ἄμ]μες ἀπέσκομεν,

οὐκ ἄλσος . [χ]όρος
              ]ψόφος
              ] . . . οιδιαι

96

and on a soft bed
gently   you would satisfy
your longing

and how there was no
holy shrine
where we were absent,

no grove
no dance
no sound"

50

ὁ μὲν γὰρ κάλος ὄσσον ἴδην πέλεται <κάλος>,
ὁ δὲ κἄγαθος αὔτικα καὶ κάλος ἔσσεται.

49

ἠράμαν μὲν ἔγω σέθεν, Ἄτθι, πάλαι ποτά

σμίκρα μοι πάις ἔμμεν᾽ ἐφαίνεο κἄχαρις.

Beauty in a Man

A man who is beautiful is beautiful to see
but a good man at once takes on beauty.

Atthis

I loved you Atthis once long ago.

You seemed to me a little child and graceless.

41

ταὶς κάλαισιν ὔμμι νόημμα τὦμον
οὐ διάμειπτον

130

Ἔρος δηὖτέ μ᾽ ὀ λυσιμέλης δόνει,
γλυκύπικρον ἀμάχανον ὄρπετον

Her Friends

For you the beautiful ones my thought
   is unchangeable

Sweetbitter

Eros loosener of limbs once again trembles me,
a sweetbitter beast irrepressibly creeping in

22

]βλα.[
]εργον, ...λ᾽ α . .[
]ν ῥέθος δοκιμ[
]ησθαι

]ν. ἀυάδην χ [
αἰ δ]ὲ μή, χείμων[
] . οισαναλγεα [
]δε

.]. ε.[...][... κ]έλομαι σ᾽ ἀ[είδην
Γο]γγύλαν [Ἄβ]ανθι λάβοισαν ἀ . [
πᾶ]κτιν, ἆς σε δηὖτε πόθος τ . [
ἀμφιπόταται

τὰν κάλαν· ἀ γὰρ κατάγωγις αὔτα[ς σ᾽
ἐπτόαισ᾽ ἴδοισαν, ἔγω δὲ χαίρω,
καὶ γὰρ αὔτα δήπο[τ᾽] ἐμέμφ[ετ᾽ ἄγνα
Κ]υπρογέν[ηα,

ὡς ἄραμα[ι
τοῦτο τὦ[πος
β]όλλομα[ι

Return, Gongyla

A deed
your lovely face

if not, winter
and no pain

I bid you, Abanthis,
take up the lyre
and sing of Gongyla as again desire
floats around you

the beautiful. When you saw her dress
it excited you. I'm happy.
The Kypros-born once
blamed me

for praying
this word:
I want

23

   ] ἔρωτος ἠλπ[
   ]
   ὡς γὰρ ἄν]τιον εἰσίδω σ[ε.

φαίνεταί μ' οὐδ'] Ἐρμιόνα τεαύ[τα
ἔμμεναι,] ξάνθαι δ' Ἐλέναι σ' ἐίσ[κ]ην
οὐδ ἔν ἄει]κες

] . ις θνάταις, τόδε δ' ἴσ[θι,] τὰι σᾶι
]παίσαν κέ με τὰν μερίμναν
]λαισ' ἀντιδ[. .]΄[.]αθοις δὲ
   ]
   δροσόεν]τας ὄχθοις
   ]ταιν
   παν]νυχίσ[δ]ην

You Can Free Me

I hoped for love

When I look at you face to face
not even Hermioni
seems to be your equal.
I compare you to blond Helen

among mortal women.
Know that you can free me
from every care,

and stay awake all night long
on dewy riverbanks

19

]

]μενοισα[
]θ᾽ ἐν θύοισι[
]έχοισαν ἔσλ[
]

]εἰ δὲ βαισα[
]ὺ γὰρ ἴδμεν[
]ιν ἔργων
]

]δ᾽ ὐπίσσω [
κ]ἀπικυδ[
]τοδ᾽ εἴπη[

Kydro

I'm waiting
to offer you a good thing
in sacrifices

but going there
we know
is labor

later toward
Kydro say
I am coming

96

]Σαρδ.[...]
πόλ]λακι τυίδε.[ν]ῶν ἔχοισα

ὤσπ.[...].ώομεν,.[..].. χ[..]-
σε θέαι σ᾽ ἰκέλαν ἀρι-
γνώται, σᾶι δὲ μάλιστ᾽ ἔχαιρε μόλπαι·

νῦν δὲ Λύδαισιν ἐμπρέπεται γυναί-
κεσσιν ὥς ποτ᾽ ἀελίω
δύντος ἀ βροδοδάκτυλος σελάννα

πάντα περρέχοισ᾽ ἄστρα· φάος δ᾽ ἐπί-
σχει θάλασσαν ἐπ᾽ ἀλμύραν
ἴσως καὶ πολυανθέμοις ἀρούραις·

ἀ δ᾽ ἐέρσα κάλα κέχυται, τεθά-
λαισι δὲ βρόδα κἄπαλ᾽ ἄν-
θρυσκα καὶ μελίλωτος ἀνθεμώδης·

πόλλα δὲ ζαφοίταισ᾽ ἀγάνας ἐπι-
μνάσθεισ᾽ Ἄτθιδος ἰμέρωι
λέπταν ποι φρένα κ[ᾶ]ρ[ι σᾶι] βόρηται·

κῆθι δ᾽ ἔλθην ἀμμ.[..]... ισα τόδ᾽ οὐ
νῶντ᾽ ἀ[..]υστονυμ[...] πόλυς
γαρύει.[...]αλον[.....].ο.μέσσον·

You in Sardis

In Sardis
her thoughts turn constantly to us here,

to you like a goddess. She was happiest
in your song.

Now she shines among Lydian women
as after sunset
the rosy-fingered moon

surpasses all the stars, and her light reaches
equally across the salt sea
and over meadows steeped in flowers.

Lucent dew pours out profusely
on blooming roses,
on frail starflowers and florid honey clover.

But wandering back and forth she remembers
gentle Atthis and for your pain
a heavy yearning consumes her

but to go there
the mind
endlessly is singing

96 (lines 21–37)

ε]ὔμαρ[ες μ]ὲν οὐκ ἄμμι θέαισι μόρ-
   φαν ἐπή[ρατ]ον ἐξίσω-
σθαι συ[. .]ρο̣ς ἔχηισθ᾽ ἀ[. . .] . νίδηον

	]το[. . . .]ρατι-
μαλ[	] ε̣ρος
καὶ δ[.]μ̣[	]ος Ἀφροδίτα

	]νέκταρ ἔχευ᾽ ἀπὺ
χρυσίας [	]ναν
. . . .]απουρ̣[	]χέρσι Πείθω

        ]ες τὸ Γεραίστιον
        ]ν̣ φίλαι
        ]υστον οὐδενο[

        ]ερον ἴξο[μ

Afroditi and Desire

It is not easy for us to equal
the goddesses
in beauty of form   Adonis

desire
and
Afroditi

poured nectar from
a gold pitcher
with hands Persuasion

the Geraistion shrine
lovers
of no one

I shall enter desire

138

στᾶθι †κἄντα† φίλος
καὶ τὰν ἐπ' ὄσσοισ' ὀμπέτασον χάριν

18

<π>άν κεδ[
<ἐ>ννέπην [
γλῶσσα μ[
μυθολογῆ[σαι,

κἄνδρι. [
μεσδον[

102

Γλύκηα μᾶτερ, οὔτοι δύναμαι κρέκην τὸν ἴστον
πόθωι δάμεισα παῖδος βραδίναν δι' Ἀφροδίταν.

A Handsome Man

Stand and face me, my love,
and scatter the grace in your eyes

Myths

All would
say
that my tongue
tells tales

and for a greater
man

Paralysis

Sweet mother, now I cannot work the loom.
Sleek Afroditi broke me with longing for a boy.

62

ἐπτάξατε[
δάφνας ὄτα[

πὰν δ᾽ ἄδιον[
ἢ κῆνον ἐλο[

καὶ ταῖσι μὲν ἀ[
ὀδοίπορος ἄν[. . . .] . . [

μύγις δέ ποτ᾽ εἰσάιον· ἐκλ[
ψύχα δ᾽ ἀγαπάτασυ [

τέαυτα δὲ νῦν ἔμμ[
ἴκεσθ᾽ ἀγανα[

ἔφθατε· κάλαν[
τά τ᾽ ἔμματα κα[

Behind a Laurel Tree

You lay in wait
behind a laurel tree

and everything
was sweeter

women
wandering

I barely heard
darling soul

such as I now am
you came

beautiful
in your garments

160

　　　τάδε νῦν ἑταίραις
ταὶς ἔμαις †τέρπνα† κάλως ἀείσω

142

Λάτω καὶ Νιόβα μάλα μὲν φίλαι ἦσαν ἔταιραι

Companions

For my companions,
now of these things I shall sing beautifully

Lito and Niobi

Lito and Niobi were deep friends

88a (lines 5–11, 13–17, 19–20, 22–24); b (line 15)

(a)] . θέλοις. οὐδυ[
] . ἀσδοισ᾽ ὀλιγα[
]ένα φέρεσθα[ι

] . φια τισ . . . [
] . δ᾽ ἄδιον εἰσορ[
ο]ἶσθα καὖτα·

λέ]λαθ᾽ ἀλλονιά[

]αἴ τις εἴποι

           ] . σαν· ἔγω τε γαρ[
(b) φιλη   ]μ᾽ ἄς κεν ἔνηι μ᾽[
           ]αι μελήσην·

]φίλα φαῖμ᾽ ἐχύρα γέ[νεσθαι

] . . . δ᾽ ὀνιαρ[.]ς[

] . πίκρος ὐμ[

] . α τόδε δ᾽ ἴσ[θ

] . ὤττι σ᾽ ἐ . [
]α φιλήσω[

118

As Long As There Is Breath

You might wish
a little
to be carried off

Someone
sweeter
you also know

forgot

and would say
yes
I shall love   as long as there is breath in me
and care
I say I have been a strong lover

hurt
bitter
and know this

no matter
I shall love

25   INCERT.

ὡς δὲ πάις πεδὰ μάτερα πεπτερύγωμαι·

Return

I have flown to you like a child to her mother.

WEATHERCOCKS
AND EXILE

158

σκιδναμένας ἐν στήθεσιν ὄργας
μαψυλάκαν γλῶσσαν πεφύλαχθαι

26 (lines 1–5, 9–12)

]θαμέω[
ὄ]ττινα[ς γὰρ
εὖ θέω, κῆνοί με μά]λιστα πά[ντων
σίνοντα]ι

] ἀλεμάτ[

] σέ, θέλω[
]τοπάθη[
] αν, ἔγω δ᾽ ἔμ᾽ [αὔται
τοῦτο συ]νοίδα

Fury

When anger is flooding through your chest
best to quiet your reckless barking tongue

Abuse

Often
those
I treat well are just the ones
who most harm me
vainly

You I want
to suffer
In me
I know it

144

> μάλα δὴ κεκορημένοις
Γόργως

133a, b

ἔχει μὲν Ἀνδρομέδα κάλαν ἀμοίβαν...

Ψάπφοι, τί τὰν πολύολβον Ἀφροδίταν...;

Gorgo

By now they have had enough of Gorgo

Andromeda

Andromeda in a beautiful exchange,

"Psapfo, why ignore Afroditi rich in blessings?"

131

Ἄτθι, σοὶ δ᾽ ἔμεθεν μὲν ἀπήχθετο
φροντίσδην, ἐπὶ δ᾽ Ἀνδρομέδαν πόται

129a, b

ἔμεθεν δ᾽ ἔχηισθα λάθαν

ἦ τιν᾽ ἄλλον ἀνθρώπων ἔμεθεν φίληισθα

Atthis Disappearing

Atthis, now the mere thought of me
is hateful and you fly off to Andromeda

Where Am I?

But you have forgotten me

or you love some man more than me

5a, b, c INCERT.

(a) †δ᾽ ἀλλ᾽ ἄν μοι† μεγαλύνεο δακτυλίωι πέρι

(b) ἄλλαν †μὴ καμετέραν† φρένα

(c) ἄβρα †δεῦτε πάσχης πάλαι† ἀλλόμαν

A Ring

Crazy woman
why are you bragging to me about a ring?

Madden

Don't madden
my mind

Delicate Girl

Delicate girl
once again
I leaped
and wandered

57

†τίς δ' ἀγροΐωτις θέλγει νόον . . .
ἀγροΐωτιν ἐπεμμένα στόλαν . . .†
οὐκ ἐπισταμένα τὰ βράκε' ἔλκην ἐπὶ τῶν σφύρων;

155

πόλλα μοι τὰν Πωλυανάκτιδα παῖδα χαίρην

Andromeda, What Now?

What farm girl dolled up in a farm dress
captivates your wits
not knowing how to pull her rags down to her ankles?

Hello and Goodbye

A hearty good day to the daughter of the house
    of Polyanax

71

οὐδὲ θέ]μις σε Μίκα
]ελα[. . αλ]λά σ᾽ ἔγωὐκ ἐάσω
]ν φιλότ[ατ᾽] ἤλεο Πενθιλήαν
]δα κα[κό]τροπ᾽, ἄμμα[
] μέλ[ος] τι γλύκερον. [
]α μελλιχόφων[ος
ἀεί]δει, λίγυραι δ᾽ ἄη[δοι
] δροσ[ό]εσσα[

Mika

You have done wrong, Mika,
I won't allow you to

faithless you chose love in the house
of Penthilos

A sweet song
in honey voice
sings
clear nightingales
over dew fields

137

θέλω τί τ᾽ εἴπην, ἀλλά με κωλύει
αἴδως ...
...
αἰ δ᾽ ἦχες ἔσλων ἴμερον ἢ κάλων
καὶ μή τί τ᾽ εἴπην γλῶσσ᾽ ἐκύκα κάκον,
αἴδως †κέν σε οὐκ† ἦχεν ὄππατ᾽
ἀλλ᾽ ἔλεγες †περὶ τῶ δικαίω†

37

κὰτ ἔμον στάλαχμον

τὸν δ᾽ ἐπιπλάζοντ᾽ ἄνεμοι φέροιεν
καὶ μελέδωναι

Alkaios Speaks and Psapfo Responds

"I want to say something to you but shame
disarms me"

"If you longed for the good or beautiful
and your tongue were not concocting evil,
shame would not cover your eyes.
Rather you would speak about the just,"

In My Pain

My pain drips

May terrifying winds carry off him
who blames me

98b

σοὶ δ᾽ ἔγω Κλέι ποικίλαν
οὐκ ἔχω πόθεν ἔσσεται
μίτϱάν<αν>· ἀλλὰ τῶι Μυτιληνάωι
                ].[
παι.α.ειον ἔχην πο.[
αἰκε.η ποικιλασκ....[

ταῦτα τὰς Κλεανακτίδα[ν
φύγας.†..ισαπολισεχει†
μνάματ᾽.. ἴδε γὰϱ αἶνα διέϱϱυε[ν

From Her Exile

For you Kleis I have no embroidered
headband and no idea
where to find one while the Mytilinian rules

These colorfully embroidered
headbands

these things of the children of the Kleanax
In exile
memories terribly wasted away

5

Κύπρι καὶ] Νηρήιδες ἀβλάβη[ν μοι
τὸν κασί]γνητον δ[ό]τε τυίδ᾽ ἴκεσθαι
κὤσσα ϝ]οι θύμωι κε θέληι γένεσθαι
πάντα τε]λέσθην,

ὄσσα δὲ πρ]όσθ᾽ ἄμβροτε πάντα λῦσα[ι
καὶ φίλοισ]ι ϝοῖσι χάραν γένεσθαι
κὠνίαν ᾽ε]χθροισι, γένοιτο δ᾽ ἄμμι
πῆμ᾽ ἔτι μ]ηδ᾽ εἶς·

τὰν κασιγ]νήταν δὲ θέλοι πόησθαι
ἔμμορον] τίμας, [ὀν]ίαν δὲ λύγραν
]οτοισι π[ά]ροιθ᾽ ἀχεύων
]. να
].εἰσαΐω[ν] τὸ κέγχρω
]λ᾽ ἐπαγ[ορί]αι πολίταν
]λλωσ[...]νηκε δ᾽ αὖτ᾽ οὐ
]κρω[

οναικ[   ]εο[   ].ι
] ... [.]ν· σὺ [δ]ὲ Κύπ[ρ]ι σ[έμ]να
]θεμ[έν]α κάκαν [
].ι.

140

Protect My Brother Haraxos

O Kypris and Nereids, I pray you
to sail my brother home unharmed
and let him accomplish all
    that is in his heart

and be released from former error
and carry joy to his friends
and bane to enemies and let no one
    bring us more grief.

Let him honor me his sister.
But black torment
    suffering for early days,

citizens accused.
Was it over millet seed?

Pure Kypris, put aside
old anger and free him from
    evil sorrow

3

]δώσην

κ]λύτων μέντ᾽ ἐπ[
κ]άλων κἄσλων, σ[
τοὶς φίλοις, λύπηις τέ μ[ε
]μ᾽ ὄνειδος

]οιδήσαις. ἐπιτ. [
]᾽αν, ἄσαιο. τὸ γὰρ ν[όημα
τῶ]μον οὐκ οὕτω μ[
]διάκηται,

]μηδ[ ]. αζε, [
]χις, συνίημ[ι
]. ης κακότατο[ς
]μεν

]ν ἀτέραις με[
]η φρένας, εὔ[
]ατοις μάκα[ρας

142

To My Brother Haraxos

By giving

good fame
your beauty and nobility
to such friends
you sicken me with pain

Blame you? Swollen
Have your fill of them
For my thinking it is poorly done
and all night I understand baseness

Other
minds
the blessed

15

]α μάκαι[ρα
]ευπλο·[
].ατοσκα[
]

ὄσσα δὲ πρ]όσθ᾽[ἄμ]βροτε κῆ[να λῦσαι
]αταις [ ]νεμ[
σὺν]τύχαι λίμ[ ]ενος κλ[
[.]
Κύ]πρι κα[ί σ]ε πι[κροτάτ]αν ἐπεύρ[οι
μη]δὲ καυχάσ[α]ι̣το τόδ᾽ ἐννέ[ποισα
Δ]ωρίχα τὸ δεύ[τ]ερον ὡς πόθε[ννον
εἰς] ἔρον ἦλθε.

7

Δωρί]χας. [. . . . . .] . [
]κην κέλετ᾽, οὐ γὰρ[
]αις
]κάνην αγερωχία[
]μμεν ὄαν νέοισι
] . αν φ[ι]λ[. . . .] . [
]μα.[

144

To Afroditi About Her Brother's Lover

Blessed one

May he be released from his past wrongs
with luck
now in harbor

Kypris, may she feel your sharp needles
and may she Doriha not go on crowing
how he came back a second time
to his desired love.

Doriha

Doriha
commands them
not to come

she is arrogant
like young men
who are loved

SECRET OF
MY CRAFT

118

ἄγι δὴ χέλυ δῖα †μοι λέγε†
φωνάεσσα †δὲ γίνεο†

32

αἴ με τιμίαν ἐπόησαν ἔργα
τὰ σφὰ δοῖσαι

Holy Tortoise Shell

Come holy lyre speak to me
and become a voice!

Some Honored Me

Some honored me by giving me
the secret of their works

53

βροδοπάχεες ἄγναι Χάριτες δεῦτε Δίος κόραι

106

πέρροχος, ὡς ὄτ' ἄοιδος ὁ Λέσβιος ἀλλοδάποισιν

Graces

Holy Graces with arms of roses,
come to me, daughters of Zeus

Singer

Towering is the Lesbian singer
compared to those in other lands

128

δεῦτέ νυν ἄβραι Χάριτες καλλίκομοί τε Μοῖσαι

127

δεῦρο δηὗτε Μοῖσαι χρύσιον λίποισαι . . .

Graces and Muses

Come to me now tender Graces
and Muses with beautiful hair

The Muses

Muses come here again to me
leaving the gold house

148

ὁ πλοῦτος ἄνευ †ἀρέτας οὐκ ἀσίνης πάροικος

ἀ δ' ἀμφοτέρων κρᾶσις †εὐδαιμονίας ἔχει τὸ ἄκρον†

56

οὐδ' ἴαν δοκίμωμι προσίδοισαν φάος ἀλίω

ἔσσεσθαι σοφίαν πάρθενον εἰς οὐδένα πω χρόνον

τεαύταν

Happiness

Wealth without virtue is no harmless neighbor
but by mixing both you are on the peak of joy.

Light

I cannot imagine in the future any girl
who looks on the light of the sun
who will have your skill and wisdom.

SANDAL

166

φαῖσι δή ποτα Λήδαν ὑακίνθινον
... ὤιον εὔρην πεπυκάδμενον

156, 167

πόλυ πάκτιδος ἀδυμελεστέρα ...
χρύσω χρυσοτέρα ...

ὠίω πόλυ λευκότερον

A Swan's Egg Containing Kastor and Polydeukis

They say that Lida once found an egg
hidden and the color of hyacinth

Comparisons

Far sweeter in sound than a lyre
more golden than gold

far whiter than an egg

135

τί με Πανδίονις, Ὤιρανα, χελίδων...;

152

παντοδάπαισι μεμειχμένα χροίαισιν

A Swallow

O Irana, why is king Pandion's daughter
now a swallow waking me?

Jason's Cloak

A mingling of all kinds of colors

92

πέπλον
[. . .] πυσχ
καὶ κλε[. .] σαω[
κροκοεντα[
πέπλον πορφυ[ρ . . . .]δεξω[.]
χλαιναι περς[
στέφανοι περ[
καλ[.]ο̣ς̣σαμ̣[
φρυ[
πορφ[υρ
τα̣π̣α̣[

Robe

robe
colored with saffron

purple robe
cloak

garland crowns
beauty

Phrygian purple
rugs

143

χρύσειοι δ' ἐρέβινθοι ἐπ' ἀιόνων ἐφύοντο

101

χερρόμακτρα δὲ †καγγόνων†
πορφύραι καταΰτμενα
†τατιμάσεις† ἔπεμψ' ἀπὺ Φωκάας
δῶρα τίμια †καγγόνων†

82a

εὐμορφοτέρα Μνασιδίκα τὰς ἀπάλας Γυρίννως

Chickpeas

Gold broom grew on riverbanks

Purple Handcloth

These purple handcloths
perfumed
she sent you from Phokaia
are expensive gifts

Beauty of Her Friends

Mnasidika is more beautifully formed
than even soft Gyrinno

81

]απύθεσ.[

]χισταλ[
]εμπ[

σὺ δὲ στεφάνοις, ὦ Δίκα, πέρθεσθ᾽ ἐράτοις φόβαισιν
ὄρπακας ἀνήτω συν<α>έρραισ᾽ ἀπάλαισι χέρσιν·

εὐάνθεα †γὰρ πέλεται† καὶ Χάριτες μάκαιραι
μᾶλλον ποτόρην, ἀστεφανώτοισι δ᾽ ἀπυστρέφονται.

On Going Bareheaded

Rebuff other ways
as quickly as you can

and you, Dika, with your soft hands take stems
of lovely anise and loop them in your locks.

The blessed Graces love to gaze at one in flowers
but turn their backs on one whose hair is bare.

39

πόδας δὲ
ποίκιλος μάσλης ἐκάλυπτε, Λύδι-
ον κάλον ἔργον

100

ἀμφὶ δ᾽ ἄβροισ᾽ ... λασίοισ᾽ εὖ <F᾽>ἐπύκασσε ...

Sandal

Colorful straps covered
her feet
in beautiful Lydian work

Garment

She was wrapped all around with a delicate
woven cloth

DREAM
AND SLEEP

6   (lines 7, 8, 10, 11, 14)

στεῖχ[ε
ὡς ἴδω[μεν
πότνια [δ᾽ Αὔως

]χρυσόπ[αχυς
]κᾶρα . [

126

δαύοις ἀπάλας ἐτα<ί>ρας ἐν στήθεσιν

Dawn with Gold Arms

Go
so we can see
Lady Dawn
with gold arms.
Doom

Sleep

May you sleep
on your tender girlfriend's breasts

149, 151

ὄτα πάννυχος ἄσφι κατάγρει

ὀφθάλμοις δὲ μέλαις νύκτος ἄωρος . . .

134

ζά <τ̓> ἐλεξάμαν ὄναρ Κυπρογένηα

Black Sleep

When all night long
           sleep closes down

and the eyes the black sleep of night

In a Dream

In a dream I talked with you born in Kypros

63

Ὄνοιρε μελαινα[
φ[ο]ίταις ὄτα τ᾽ ὔπνος [

γλύκυς θ[έ]ος, ἦ δεῖν᾽ ὀνίας μ[
ζὰ χῶρις ἔχην τὰν δυναμ[

ἔλπις δέ μ᾽ ἔχει μὴ πεδέχη[ν
μηδὲν μακάρων ἐλ[

οὐ γάρ κ᾽ ἔον οὔτω[. .
ἀθύρματα κα [
γένοιτο δέ μοι[
τοὶς πάντα[

Dream

O dream on black wings
you stray here when sleep

sweet god, I am in agony
to split all its power

for I expect not to share.
Nothing of the blessed gods

I would rather not be like this
with trinkets

but may
I have them all

120

ἀλλά τις οὐκ ἔμμι παλιγκότων
ὄργαν, ἀλλ᾽ ἀβάκην τὰν φρέν᾽ ἔχω …

70   (lines 3, 7, 9–11, 13)

]ν̣δ᾽ εἶμ᾽ ε[
]ς̣ γὰρ ἐπαυ[
]αρμονίας δ[
]αθην χόρον, ἄα[
]δε λίγηα ̣[
]παντεσσι[

Innocence

I am not of a wounding spirit
rather I have a gentle heart

Clear Voiced

I will go
hear
harmony
dance choir
clear voiced
to all

73a

]αν Ἀφροδί[τα
ἀ]δύλογοι δ᾽ ἐρ[
]βαλλοι
]ις ἔχοισα
] ἔνα θαασ[σ
]άλλει
]ας ἐέρσας[

4

]θε θῦμον
]μι πάμπαν
] δύναμαι,
]

]ας κεν ἦ μοι
]ς ἀντιλάμπην
]λον πρόσωπον.
]

]γχροΐσθεις
] ᾽ [..]ρος

Dew

Afroditi
soft-worded desires
hurl
holding
a seat

flourishing
lovely
dew

Face

Now in my
heart I
see clearly

a beautiful
face
shining back on me,

stained
with love

AGE AND LIGHT

85

```
    ] . .              ] πάμενα[
 `] λβον            ] τ' ὧστ' ὀ πέλη[
]ακούην            ] ακαν σό[
]αύταν
```

139

θέοι δ[. . .] . νεσω . [. . α]ὔτικ' ἀδάκ[ρυτον
θε[

150

οὐ γὰρ θέμις ἐν μοισοπόλων †οἰκίαι†
θρῆνον ἔμμεν· οὔ κ᾽ ἄμμι πρέποι τάδε.

Old Man

Rich
like listening to
an old man

Gods

Among gods
right off
the one
who sheds
no tears

*Angry with Her Daughter When
She Psapfo Was Dying*

It is not right in a house serving the Muses
to have mourning. For us it is unbecoming.

21

] επαβολης[
]ανδ᾽ ὄλοφυν [. . .]ε .
] τρομέροις π . [. . .]αλλα
]

] χρόα γῆρας ἤδη
]ν ἀμφιβάσκει
]ς πέταται διώκων
]

]τας ἀγαύας
]εα, λάβοισα
] ἄεισον ἄμμι
τὰν ἰόκολπον.   ]

]ρων μάλιστα
]ας π[λ]άναται

Old Age

In pity
and
trembling

old age now
covers my flesh.
Yet there is chasing and floating

after a young woman.
Pick up your lyre
and sing to us

of one with violets
on her robe, especially
wandering

147

μνάσασθαί τινά φαιμι †καὶ ἕτερον† ἀμμέων.

95

Γογγυλα . [

ἦ τι σᾶμ᾽ ἐθε [
παισι μάλιστα . [
μας γ᾽ εἴσηλθ᾽ ἐπ . [

εἶπον· ὦ δέσποτ᾽, ἐπ . [
ο]ὐ μὰ γὰρ μάκαιραν [ἔγωγ᾽
ο]ὐδὲν ἄδομ᾽ ἔπερθα γᾶ[ς ἔοισα,

κατθάνην δ᾽ ἴμερός τις [ἔχει με καὶ
λωτίνοις δροσόεντας [ὄ-
χ[θ]οισ ἴδην Ἀχέρ[οντος

No Oblivion

Someone, I tell you, in another time,
will remember us.

To Hermis Who Guides the Dead

Gongyla

surely a sign
especially for children
who came here

I said, O master   by the blessed
Afroditi   I swear I take no pleasure
in being on the earth

but a longing seizes me to die
and see the dewy
lotus banks of the Aheron

55

κατθάνοισα δὲ κείσηι οὐδέ ποτα μναμοσύνα σέθεν
ἔσσετ᾽ οὐδὲ πόθα εἰς ὕστερον· οὐ γὰρ πεδέχηις
   βρόδων
τὼν ἐκ Πιερίας· ἀλλ᾽ ἀφάνης κἀν Ἀίδα δόμωι
φοιτάσηις πεδ᾽ ἀμαύρων νεκύων ἐκπεποταμένα.

27   INCERT. (1)

κ]αδδέκεται μέλαινα[
   ]ων ἀχέων ἐπαύσθη[
   ]... ἴδαι. λεεοι. [

190

To a Woman of No Education

When you lie dead no one will remember
or long for you later. You do not share the roses
of Pieria. Unseen here and in the house of Hades,
flown away, you will flitter among dim corpses.

Menelaos

He lies received in the black earth,
a son of Atreus,
released now from his agony.

18b, c   INCERT.

<   > ὀνίαν τε κὐγιείαν…
<   > σα φύγοιμι, παῖδες, ἄβα…

121

ἀλλ᾿ ἔων φίλος ἄμμι
λέχος ἄρνυσο νεώτερον·
οὐ γὰρ τλάσομ᾿ ἔγω συνοί-
κην ἔοισα γεραιτέρα

Wish

Both distress and good health

My children, let me fly back
youth

Age and the Bed

Really, if you are my friend,
             choose a younger bed

I can't bear to live with you
             when I am the older

65

[.....]πυφα[

[.. Ἀνδ]ρομε[δ.

[.....]δελασ [

.]ροτήννεμε[
Ψάπφοι, σὲ φίλ[ημμ᾽

Κύπρωι βασίληα[
καί τοι μέγα δ. [

ὄ]σσοις φαέθων ἀ[έλιος
πάνται κλέος [

καί σ᾽ ἐνν Ἀχέρ[οντ
[.]ρ[......]νπ[

194

Afroditi to Psapfo

Andromeda
forgot

but Psapfo
I loved you

In Kypros I am queen
for you a power

as sun blazes
glory everywhere;

even by the Aheron I am with you

58b CAMPBELL (lines 11–12)
MARTIN WEST (TLS 6.24.05)
from a Cologne papyrus

Ὗμμες πεδὰ Μοίσαν ἰ]οκ[ό]λπων κάλα δῶρα, παῖδες,
σπουδάσδετε καὶ τὰ]ν φιλάοιδον λιγύραν χελύνναν·

ἔμοι δ᾽ ἄπαλον πρίν] ποτ᾽ [ἔ]οντα χρόα γῆρας ἤδη
ἐπέλλαβε, λεῦκαι δ᾽ ἐγ]ένοντο τρίχες ἐκ μελαίναν·

βάρυς δέ μ᾽ ὀ [θ]ῦμος πεπόηται, γόνα δ᾽ [ο]ὐ φέροισι,
τὰ δή ποτα λαίψηρ᾽ ἔον ὄρχησθ᾽ ἴσα νεβρίοισι.

τὰ <μὲν> στεναχίσδω θαμέως· ἀλλὰ τί κεν ποείην;
ἀγήραον ἄνθρωπον ἔοντ᾽ οὐ δύνατον γένεσθαι.

καὶ γάρ π[ο]τα Τίθωνον ἔφαντο βροδόπαχυν Αὖων
ἔρωι φ. αθεισαν βάμεν᾽ εἰς ἔσχατα γᾶς φέροισα[ν,

ἔοντα [κ]άλον καὶ νέον, ἀλλ᾽ αὖτον ὔμως ἔμαρψε
χρόνωι πόλιον γῆρας, ἔχ[ο]ντ᾽ ἀθανάταν ἄκοιτιν.

196

Growing Old*

Those lovely gifts of the fragrant-breasted Muses,
girls, seek them eagerly in thrilling song of the lyre.

Old age has grasped my earlier delicate skin
and my black hair has become white,

my spirit turned heavy, my knees no longer
carry me nimble for dancing like a fawn.

About these things I groan. What can I do?
For a human not to grow old is impossible.

They say Dawn, dazzled by love, took Tithonos
in her rose arms to the utter end of the earth.

Once beautiful and young, time seized him
into gray old age, husband of a deathless wife.

* Translated by Willis Barnstone and William McCulloh.

58c   (lines 25–26)

ἔγω δὲ φίλημμ' ἀβροσύναν,   ] τοῦτο καί μοι
τὸ λά[μπρον ἔρος τὠελίω καὶ τὸ κά]λον λέ[λ]ογχε.

Desire and Sun

Yet I love refinement and Eros has got me
brightness and the beauty of the sun.

INDIRECT
POEMS

201

φησὶν ἡ Σαπφὼ ὅτι τὸ ἀποθνήισκειν κακόν·
οἱ θεοὶ γὰρ οὕτω κεκρίκασιν· ἀπέθνηισκον γὰρ ἄν.

ARISTOTLE, *RHETORIC* 1398B

204

ὁ δὲ χρυσὸς ἄφθαρτος

SCHOLIAST ON PINDAR'S
PYTHIAN ODES 4.410C
(II. 153 DRACHMANN)

Death Is Evil

Death is evil. So the gods decided.
Otherwise they would die.

ARISTOTLE, *RHETORIC* 1398B

Gold

Gold is indestructible.

SCHOLIAST ON PINDAR'S
PYTHIAN ODES 4.410C
(II.153 DRACHMANN)

ELEGIAC POEMS
FROM THE
Greek Anthology
WRONGLY
ATTRIBUTED
TO SAPPHO

159 DIEHL

τῶι γριπεῖ Πελάγωνι πατὴρ ἐπέθηκε Μενίσκος
κύρτον καὶ κώπαν, μνᾶμα κακοζοΐας.

158 DIEHL

Τιμάδος ἅδε κόνις, τὰν δὴ πρὸ γάμοιο θανοῦσαν
δέξατο Φερσεφόνας κυάνεος θάλαμος,
ἇς καὶ ἀποφθιμένας πᾶσαι νεοθᾶγι σιδάρωι
ἅλικες ἱμερτὰν κρατὸς ἔθεντο κόμαν.

On Pelagon

Pelagon the fisherman. His father Meniskos left here
    his basket and oar, relics of a wretched life.

On Timas

Here is the dust of Timas who unmarried
    was led into Persefoni's dark bedroom,
and when she died her girlfriends took sharp
    iron knives and cut off their soft hair.

TESTIMONIA AND ENCOMIA

TESTIMONIA, FROM THE *plural of the Latin* testimonium, *refers to the extant biographical, critical, and literary references to Sappho in Greek and Latin antiquity. Except for the famous line to Sappho by her contemporary Lesbian poet Alkaios, "O violet-haired, holy, honeysmiling Sappho," the earliest testimonia date from no earlier than a century after Sappho's death.*

Biographical Information and Information Said to Be in Sappho's Poems

Sappho was born on Lesbos and lived in the city of Mytilini. Her father was Skamandros, or according to some, Skamandronymos. She had three brothers, Eurygios, Larihos, and Haraxos, the oldest, who sailed to Egypt and became the lover of Doriha, on whom he spent much money. Since Larihos was the youngest, Sappho loved him most. She had a daughter named Kleis who was named after Sappho's mother. She was accused by some writers of being irregular in her way of life and a woman-lover. In appearance she seems to have been contemptible and ugly. [Socrates called her "the beautiful Sappho."] She had a dark complexion and was very short. The same is true of . . . [Alkaios?], who was smallish. . . . She used the Aiolic dialect . . . wrote nine books of lyric poetry and one of elegiac forms.

Papyri Oxyrhynchus 1800 frag. 1

Sappho was the daughter of Simon or Euminos or Ierigyios or Ekrytos or Simos or Kamon or Etarhos or Skamandronymos. Her mother was Kleis. A Lesbian from Eressos and a lyric poet, she lived in the forty-second Olympiad [612–608 B.C.E.], when Alkaios, Stisihoros and Pittakos were also alive. She had three brothers, Larihos, Haraxos, and Eurygios. She married Kerkylas, a very rich man from Andros, and had a daughter by him named Kleis. She had three companions and friends, Atthis, Telesippa, and Megara, and she was slandered for having a shameful friendship with them. Her students were Anagora of Militos, Gongyla of Kolofon, and Euneika of Salamis. She wrote nine books of lyric poetry and invented the plectrum (pick) for playing the lyre. She also wrote epigrams, elegaics, iambic poems, and monodies.

The Suda Lexicon 107A (4.322s ADLER)

The poet Sappho, daughter of Skamandronymos. Even Plato, son of Ariston, calls her wise and skillful. I understand that there was also another Sappho of Lesbos who was a courtesan, not a poet.

Ailios Aristides *Historical Miscellanies* 12.19 (P. 135 DILTS)

Sappho, a lyric poet, daughter of Skamandronymos and a native of Mytilini.

Scholiast on Plato's *Phaidros* 235C

The beautiful Sappho. Socrates liked to call her this because of the beauty of her song, although she was small and dark.

Maximus of Tyre, *Orations* 24(18)7

Physically, Sappho was very ugly, small and dark, and one can only describe her as a nightingale with deformed wings enfolding a tiny body.

Scholiast on Lucian's Portraits 18

The renowned poets Sappho and Alkaios lived in the Olympiad 45.2 (598 B.C.E.).

Eusebios Chronicle

From the time Sappho sailed from Mytilini to Sicily when she was exiled in the years . . . [605/4–591—perhaps for the second time]. This was when Kritias was the archon at Athens and during the rule of the Gamori [landowners] at Syracuse [598 B.C.E.].

Parian Marble Chronicle EP. 36 (P. 12 JACOBY)

Here Hermesianax is wrong in making Sappho a contemporary of Anakreon's. For he belongs to the time of Cyrus and Polykrates, while Sappho is a contemporary of Alyattes, father of Kroisos.

Athinaios Scholars at Dinner 599C

Sappho was a Lesbian from Mytilini and a lyre player. She threw herself down from the Leukadian Cliff out of love for Phaon of Mytilini. Some say that she composed poetry.

The Suda Lexicon 107 (IV 322 ADLER)

You are a Phaon both in beauty and deeds. This proverb is used for those who are handsome and proud. They say that Sappho, among many others, was in love with Phaon, but she was not the poet Sappho but another Lesbian, who,

having failed in winning his love, leaped from the Leuka-
dian Cliff.

The Suda Lexicon: Phaon

Phaon, a ferryman who made his living sailing back and forth
between Lesbos and the mainland, one day took Venus, in the
guise of an old woman, over for nothing. She gave him an ala-
baster box of unguents, which he used daily to make women
fall in love with him. Among them was one who in her frustra-
tion was said to have jumped from Mount Leukates, and from
this story came the present custom of hiring people once a
year to jump into the sea from that place.

Servius on Virgil's *Aeneid* 10.452

The island of Leukas has the temple of Apollo Leukates and a
ledge for a leap from which one can cure love. Menandros
says,

> Sappho was the first to leap from the prominent rock
> in her madly amorous pursuit of the proud Phaon.
> But now by my vow, I shall praise your sacred
> precinct on the Leukadian Cliff, O Lord Apollo.

Although Menandros assigns Sappho priority in jumping, the
more skilled authorities say it was Kephalos who was in love
with Pterelas, son of Deioneus. It was an annual custom of the
Leukadians to throw some guilty person from the cliff during
the sacrifice to Apollo in order to avert evil; they tied all kinds
of birds and winged creatures to him so that they might brake
his fall by their fluttering, and a large crowd waited for him
underneath in small boats to save him, if possible, in that area
outside the sacred precinct.

Strabon *Geography* 10.2.9 (2.348 KRAMER)

Later the actual promontory seems to have been known as Aiga [the "goat"], as Sappho calls it, and later as Kane and Kanai.

Strabon Geography 13.615

It is said that this pyramid was built by her lovers as a tomb for a prostitute who is called Doriha by the lyric poet Sappho. She became the mistress of Sappho's brother Haraxos when he visited Naukratis with a cargo of Lesbian wine; others call her Rodopis.

Strabon Geography 17.1.33 (3.379 KRAMER)

Rodopis was brought to Egypt by Xanthous the Samian to ply her trade, and Haraxos of Mytilini, son of Skamandronymos and brother of the poet Sappho, paid a large sum to redeem her from slavery. It seems that Naukratis must be a good place for beautiful prostitutes, for not only did Rodopis live there and become so famous that every Greek was familiar with her name. . . . When Haraxos returned to Mytilini after setting Rodopis free, he was ridiculed by Sappho in one of her poems.

Herodotos Histories 2.135

Naukratis produced some famous and outstandingly beautiful courtesans. Doriha became Haraxos's mistress when he went to Naukratis on a business trip, and beautiful Sappho accuses her in a poem of having fleeced her brother Haraxos of much of his fortune. But Herodotos calls her Rodopis (instead of Doriha) since he does not know that she is not the same woman who dedicated the famous spits at Delphi, which Kratinos mentions. The following epigram was written by Poseidippos, who speaks of her many times in the *Aisopeia*:

> Doriha, your bones are covered now
> by only a headband for your soft hair

and also by the perfumed robe in
which you once wrapped your graceful
Haraxos while embracing him until
it was time for the morning wine.
But the white speaking pages of Sappho's
dear song remain. Blessed is your name
which Naukratis will preserve as long
as any ship sails the shallow Nile.

Another beautiful courtesan was Archedike of Nau-
kratis. . . . According to Nymphis in his *Voyage Around Asia*, the
courtesan of Eressos who was a namesake of the other Sappho
became famous as the lover of beautiful Phaon.

The poem is Poseidippos 17, *Aisopeia*,
quoted in Athinaios, *Scholars at Dinner*, 13.596B

What else could one call the Lesbian's love but that which
Socrates practiced. Both seem to me to have practiced love in
their own way, she of women, he of men, and both said that
they could fall in love many times and all beautiful people
attracted them. What Alkibiadis, Harmides, and Phaidros
were to him, Gyrinna, Atthis, and Anaktoria were to her;
and what his rival philosophers Prodikos, Gorgias, Thra-
symahos, and Protagoras were to Socrates, so Gorgo and
Andromeda were to Sappho, who sometimes rebuked them,
at others refuted them and spoke ironically to them just as
Socrates did to his rivals. [See Sources 155.]

Maximus of Tyre *Orations* 24.18.9 (P. 230s HOBEIN)

The grammarian Didymus wrote four thousand books. I
would pity anyone who simply had to read so many su-
premely empty works. Among his books he inquires about

the birthplace of Homer, the real mother of Aeneas, whether Anakreon was more of a lecher than a drunkard, whether Sappho was a prostitute, and other things which you ought to forget if you knew them. And then people complain that life is short.

Seneca Letters to Lucilius E P. 88

And do you think that refinement without virtue is desirable? Why, Sappho, who was a true woman and a poet, had too much reverence to separate honor from refinement, for she says:

> Yet I love refinement and Eros has got me
> brightness and the beauty of the sun.

She made it clear to all that her desire for living included both the bright and the honorable. For these belong to virtue.

Athinaios Scholars at Dinner 15.687 (2.424 KAIBEL)

It was the custom among the ancient peoples for the young men of the noblest families to serve the wine. . . . Beautiful Sappho often praises her brother Larihos for the way he served the wine in the council hall of Mytilini.

Athinaios Scholars at Dinner 10.424E

Socrates: There are wise people from earlier times who wrote and spoke of these things and would refute me if I agreed to please you. Phaidros: Who are they? What have they said that is better? Socrates: I cannot say offhand, but it is clear that I got better information from one of the ancients, from either the beautiful Sappho or the wise Anakreon or some historian.

Plato Phaidros 235B

Socrates blazed up in anger with Xanthippe for lamenting when he was near death as Sappho did with her daughter.

Maximus of Tyre *Orations* 24.18.9

After men were created . . . Prometheus is said to have stolen fire and revealed it to them. The gods were angered about this and sent two evils on the earth, fever [or women] and disease, as we are told by Sappho and Hesiod.

Servius on Virgil's *Eclogues* 6.42

Sappho sang many contradictory things about Eros.

Pausanias *Description of Greece* 9.27.3

Alkaios called Eros the son of Iris and Zephyros; Sappho called him the son of Afroditi and Ouranos.

Scholiast on Theokritos 13.1/2c (p. 216 WENDEL)

Sappho [said that Eros descended] from Ge [Earth] and Ouranos [Sky].

Scholiast on Apollonios of Rhodes 3.26

And it is said that Selini [the moon] goes down into that cave to meet Endymion. Sappho and Nikandros, in his book on Europa, relate the love of Selini.

Scholiast on Apollonios of Rhodes's *Argonautika* 4.57 (p. 264 WENDEL)

The *baromos* and *barbitos*, mentioned by both Sappho and Anakreon, and the *magadis*, *trigonon* [triangles] and *sambuka* are all ancient instruments.

Athinaios *Scholars at Dinner* 4.182E

Your situation may now be compared to that of the leader of the Muses himself [Apollo], as he appears when Sappho and Pindar say in their songs when they adorn him with golden hair and a lyre, and send him drawn by a team of swans to Mount Helikon to dance there with the Muses and Graces.

Himerios, Orations, 13.7 (p. 186s. Colonna)

Anakreon . . . says that anise was used for making garlands, and so do Sappho and Alkaios, and the latter also speak of celery.

Pollux Vocabulary 6.107 (2.31 Bethe)

Sappho calls Zeus by the name "the Holder."

Hesychios Lexicon E 1750 (2.56 Latte)

Sappho calls the coffer in which unguents and woman's articles are kept *gryta*.

Phrynichos Sophistic Preparation (p. 60 von Borries)

Sappho's word *beudos* is equivalent to *kimberikon*, a transparent vest.

Pollux Vocabulary 7.49 (2.65 Bethe)

Thapsos (fustic) is a wood for dying hair yellow. Sappho calls it Scythian wood.

Photios Lexicon 81.12s. (p. 274 Naber)

Pamphos, who composed the oldest hymns for the Athenians, called Linos by the name of Oitolinos [Dead Linos] at the climax of mourning for him. Sappho of Lesbos, having learned the name Oitolinos from the verses of Pamphos, sang of Adonis and Oitolinos together.

Pausanias Description of Greece 9.29.8 (3.64 SPIRO)

Menaichmos of Sikyon in his Treatise on Artists declares that Sappho was the first to use the pectis [a kind of lyre], which he says is the same as the magadis [an instrument with twenty strings].

Athinaios Scholars at Dinner 14.635B (3.401 KAIBEL)

[She was called] "manly Sappho," either because she was famous as a poet, an art in which men are known, or else because she has been defamed for being of that tribe [of homosexuals].

Porphyrio, in Horace's Epistles 1.19.28 (P. 362 HOLDER)

The statue of Sappho stolen from the town hall of Syracuse . . . so perfect, so elegant, so elaborately finished. . . . Not only was it exquisitely done, but it contained an epigram on the base.

Cicero Orations against Verres 2.4.57.125–27

Encomia and Other Comments

The sweet glory of the Lesbians.

Lucian Loves 30

A contemporary of Pittakos and Alkaios was Sappho—a marvel. In all the centuries since history began, I know of no woman who in any true sense can be said to rival her as a poet.

Strabon Geography 13.2.3 (3.65S KRAMER)

One evening, while drinking wine, the nephew of Solon the Athenian sang one of Sappho's songs, and Solon liked it so much that he ordered the boy to teach it to him. When one of the company asked why he was learning it, he answered, "I want to learn it and die."

Stobaios Anthology 3.29.58 (3.638s. WACHSMUTH-HENSE)

Everybody honors the wise. The Parians honored Archilochos despite his slanderous tongue, the Chians honored Homer though he was not a Chian, and the Mytilinians honored Sappho although she was a woman.

Aristotle Rhetoric 1398B

"Don't you see," he said, "what charm the songs of Sappho have to hold the listeners spellbound?"

Plutarch Pythian Oracles 6

We were the first to be displeased with and condemn the new custom, which was imported into Rome, of reading from Plato as an after-dinner entertainment and listening to his dialogues over the dessert, perfumes, and wine, so that now when they recite Sappho or Anakreon, I think I should put down my cup out of respect.

Plutarch Dinner-Table Problems 7.8.2

It is fitting to mention Sappho along with the Muses. The Romans speak of how Kakos, son of Hefaistos, let fire and flames flow out of his mouth. And Sappho's words are truly mixed with fire, and through her songs she brings out her heart's warmth, and according to Philoxenos heals the pain of love with the sweet-voiced Muses.

Plutarch Dialogue in Love 18

After eating, it was time for wine and conversation. Antonius Julianus desired that we might have a performance by excellent singers of both sexes whom he knew our young friend had at his disposal. And then young men and women were presented to us and they sang in a pleasant way many songs by Anakreon and Sappho and also some sweet, charmingly erotic elegies by recent composers.

Aulus Gellius Attic Nights 19.9.3s (P. 573 MARSHALL)

For these ladies consider it the highest kind of embellishment when people say that they are educated and wise and write poems almost as good as Sappho's.

Lucian On Paid Companions 36

The Mytilinians engraved Sappho on their coins.

Pollux Vocabulary 9.84

Free women and young girls even today call their intimate and loving friends *hetaira* (companions) as Sappho does [in fragments 142 and 160].

Athinaios Scholars at Dinner 13.571D

Literary Criticism

The polished and florid composition has the following characteristics. . . . It would be pertinent for me to enumerate the people who excelled in it. Among the epic poets Hesiod seems to me to have best worked out this style; and among the lyrical poets, Sappho, and with her, Anakreon and Simonides; among the tragic poets, only Euripides; among the historians, no one, to be exact, but Ephoros and Theopompos somewhat more than the others; among the orators, Isokratis. I shall now give examples of this style, selecting Sappho among the poets and Isokratis among the orators. I begin with the lyric poet: [There follows the complete poem "Prayer to Afroditi."] The euphony and charm of this passage lie in the cohesion and smoothness of the connecting phrases. For the words are juxtaposed and interwoven according to the natural affinities and unions of the letters.

Dionysios of Halikarnassos *On Literary Composition* 23

For example, Sappho takes the emotions appropriate to the passion of love from true life. And she shows her virtue when she takes the best and most excellent events and expertly selects and combines them. [There follows the poem "Seizure."] Is it not wonderful how simultaneously she summons the soul, body, hearing, tongue, sight, flesh, all as separate things distinct from herself, and by contrary elements, she both freezes and burns, is mad and sane; she is afraid or she is nearly dead; thus not only one passion is evident but a whole assembly of emotions; for all of these things happen to lovers, and her taking the best of the emotions, as I said, and joining them together, produces the excellence of this passage.

Longinos *On the Sublime* 10

Then comes the polished and decorative style, which prefers elegance to solemnity. It uses the smoothest and gentlest words, seeking euphony and musicality, from which comes its charm. It does not let words come together by chance or thoughtlessly but places each word carefully with another to reproduce the most musical sounds; it examines what arrangement will produce the most graceful combination; it attempts to put things together with regard to the coherence of the parts, rubbed down and smoothed, all the joints cleanly dove-tailed. . . . These, I believe, are the characteristics of this style. Examples of this style are Hesiod, Sappho, and Anakreon in poetry, and in prose the Athenian Isokratis and his followers.

Dionysios of Halikarnassos Demosthenes 40

Hymns of invocation are like most of the hymns of Sappho [such as "Prayer to Afroditi," 1], Anakreon, or other poets, and contain invocations of many deities . . . The poetic hymns of invocation are long. They can summon the gods from many places, as we find in Sappho and Alkman: The poets summon Artemis from many mountains, many cities, and from rivers too, and Afroditi from Kypros (Cyprus), Knidos, Syria, and many other places. And they can also describe the places themselves: in the instance of rivers, the water and the banks, the near meadows and dances performed by the rivers, and so on. Similarly, if they call them from their temples, they must be long hymns of invocation.

Menandros On Oratorical Apology
(9.132, 135S. WALZ; 3.333, 334S. SPENGEL)

If we compare Sappho's poems with Anakreon's or the Sibyl's oracles with the prophet Bakis, then it is clear that the art of poetry or of prophecy is not one art practiced by men and another art when practiced by women. It is the same. Can anyone protest this conclusion?

Plutarch Virtues of Women 243 (2.226 NACHSTÄDT)

The rites of Afroditi were left [by other poets] alone to the Lesbian Sappho for singing to the lyre and composing the epithalamium. After contests among the suitors, she enters the bridal room, weaves the bower, makes the bridal bed, gathers the virgins into the bridal chamber, and brings Afroditi in her chariot drawn by Graces and a band of Eroses to join in the fun. She braids Afroditi's hair with hyacinth, and except for the locks parted at the forehead, she leaves the rest free to float and ripple in the breezes. Then she adorns the wings and the curls of the Eroses with gold, and urges them on before the chariot, waving their torches in the air.

Himerios Orations 9.4 (P. 75s. COLONNA)

Only Sappho among women loved beauty along with the lyre, and so she dedicated all her poetry to Afroditi and Eroses, making a young woman's beauty and graces the subject of her songs.

Himerios Orations 28.2 (P. 128s. COLONNA)

She was a woman of Lesbos too, who wrote lasciviously yet with such grace that she reconciles us to her outrageous speech through the sweetness of her songs.

Apuleius, Apology 9 (P. 10 HELM)

Sappho loves the rose and always crowns it with praise, comparing the beautiful virgins to it, and she compares it to the arms of the Graces when they have left them bare.

Philostratos Letters 51

This talented woman's name was Damophyla, and it is said that she had virgin girlfriends, just as Sappho did, and that she composed love poems and hymns as Sappho did. The hymns to Artemis are derived ultimately from Sapphic models.

Philostratos Life of Apollonios of Tyana 1.30 (1.32 KAYSER)

For a second and third example we may think of the famous Theano and the Lesbian poet, and for a fourth, Diotima.

Theano contributed an idea of greatness of mind and Sappho gave us refinement.

Lucian *Portraits* 18

Anakreon of Teos was the first poet after Sappho of Lesbos to make love the main subject of his poetry.

Pausanias *Description of Greece* 1.25.1

In his second book of his *Treatise on Erotika*, Klearhos says that the love songs and Lokrian songs of Gnesippos are not different from the poems of Sappho or Anakreon.

Athinaios *Scholars at Dinner* 13.605e

We forgive the unmeasured and excessive praises given by Sappho and Anakreon to their beloved, for the loved and the lover were private people and there was no danger that they would become conceited by their praise.

Themistios *Orations* 13.170D–171A
(p. 209 Dindorf, p. 245 Downey)

Their charm may be inherent in the subject, such as the gardens of the nymphs, a wedding, love affairs, all the poetry of Sappho.

Dimitrios *On Style* 132 (p. 132 Rhy Roberts)

In a different way Sappho makes fun of the rustic bridegroom and the doorkeeper of the bridal chamber. It is a very commonplace style, pertaining more to prose than to poetry, and so it would be better for these poems to be spoken rather than to be sung. They are not suitable for the dance or the lyre except for a kind of dance conversation.

Dimitrios *On Style* 167 (p. 37 Radermacher)

The grace that comes from her use of formal devices is evident and frequent, such as the use of repetition where the bride says to her virginity: "Virginity, virginity, where have you gone, leaving me abandoned?" And she replies with the same formal device: "No longer will I come to you. No longer will I come." Far more grace is evident than if it had been said only once and this formal device had not been used. Although repetition seems to have been invented in order to show force, Sappho uses even what is very forceful with great charm.

Dimitrios *On Style* 140 (p. 33 RADERMACHER)

And this is why when Sappho sings of beauty, she is sweet and full of beautiful words, and the same holds true when she sings of love, spring, and the halcyon, and every beautiful word is woven into her poetry, and some of her own creation.

Dimitrios *On Style* 166 (p. 37 RADERMACHER)

For Homer says that she [Niobi] had six [children] of each sex, Euripides seven, Sappho nine, and Bacchylides and Pindar ten.

Aulus Gellius *Attic Nights* 20.7 (2.301 HOSIUS)

Some take this to mean that Theseus set free seven boys and seven girls, as Plato says in the *Phaidon*, Sappho in her lyric poems, Bacchylides in his dithyrambs, and Euripides in his *Herakles*.

Servius on Virgil's *Aeneid* 6.21

Since the passage of time has destroyed Sappho and her works, her lyre and her songs, before you I will set other examples.

Tzetzes *On the Meters of Pindar* 20–22 (CRAMER *AN. PAR.* 1.63)

The Mixolydian mode is especially passionate, befitting tragedy. Aristoxenos declares that this mode was invented by Sappho and that the writers of tragedy learned from her.

Plutarch On Music 16.1136C (3.13 Ziegler)

Diotima says [in Plato's *Symposium*] that Eros [love] flourishes in abundance and dies in want. Sappho put these together and called Eros "bittersweet" [literally "sweetbitter"]. [See poem 130.]

Maximus of Tyre Orations 18.9GH (P. 232 Hobein)

She was a woman of Lesbos too, who wrote lasciviously yet with such grace that she reconciles us to her outrageous speech through the sweetness of her songs.

Apuleius Apology 9 (P. 10 Helm)

Prosody*

First, the epichoriambic, also called the Sapphic eleven-syllable verse. . . . It is also found in Alkaios, but it is not clear which of the two poets invented the verse, though it is named after Sappho.

Hefaistion Handbook of Meters 43

The common form of the stanza can be described as written line by line and stanza by stanza as in the Book 2 and Book 3 of Sappho. In the ancient copies we note each song marked with the *paragraphos* two lines each, and there is no example of

---

* For a full treatment of Sappho's metrics, see professor William McCulloh's Metrical Guide, which he recently revised and expanded for this book.

an odd number of lines. We presume they were composed with the stanza as the unit. Yet since each line in the couplet is identical and it could have been by accident that Sappho made all her lines in even number of lines, one might also argue that they were composed with the line as the unit.

Hefaistion *On Poetry* 1.3 (P. 63 CONSBRUCH)

The Sapphic variety of the heroic hexameter is a line that both begins and ends with a spondee.

Scholiast on Hefaistion's *Handbook of Meters* 293

Poems are called common when they are formed of metrical systems in which the lines are of the same meter, such as in the second and third books of Sappho. In these the stanzas are two lines each and similar.

Hefaistion *Handbook of Meters* 60

The dactylic Adonian dimeter catalectic was invented by Sappho, and for this reason it is also called the monoschematist Sapphic, for it always consists of a dactyl and a spondee.

Marius Plotius Sacerdos *Art of Grammar* 6.516

From Greek Poetry on Sappho

This tomb contains the silent bones of Sappho,
but her wise sayings are immortal.

Pinytos, in *The Greek Anthology* 7.16

O stranger, when you pass my Aiolian tomb, do not say that I, the singer of Mytilini, am dead.

Human hands made this tomb, and mortal works fall
    quickly into oblivion. But compare me
to the sacred Muses, from each of whom I took one flower
    for my nine books. You'll see I have escaped
from the gloom of Hades, and each dawn the sun
    wakens the name of the lyric poet Sappho.

Tullius Laureas, in *The Greek Anthology* 7.17

Anyti has many lilies woven in the wreath, Moiro many
    white ones. Sappho has few, but roses.

Meleagros's poem in *The Greek Anthology* 4.1

My name is Sappho. My song surpasses the song
    of women as Homer's the song of men.

Antipatros of Thessaloniki, in *The Greek Anthology* 7.15

Memory was astounded when she heard
the honey-voiced Sappho, and she wondered
whether mankind had a tenth Muse.

Antipatros of Sidon, in *The Greek Anthology* 9.66

Aiolian land, you cover Sappho sung as a mortal Muse
    among the deathless Muses whom Kypris
and Eros nourished, with whom Persuasion wove
    an undying wreath of the Pierian Muses.
She was a joy to Greece and to you. You fates who twirl
    the triple thread on your spindle,
why didn't you spin eternal life for the singer inventing
    the enduring poems of Helikon's daughters?

Antipatros of Sidon, in *The Greek Anthology* 7.14

Your poems, Sappho, are the sweetest pillow
    for young lovers. Surely Pieria
or ivied Helikon honors you, whose breath is equal
    to theirs, you Muse of Aiolian Eressos.
Hymen, the wedding god, is near you when he, bright
    torch in hand, stands by the bed
of the newlywed, or Afroditi keeps you near as she
    mourns the young offspring of Adonis
in the sacred grove of the blessed. I greet you as a god.
    Your songs are our immortal daughters.

Dioskorides, in The Greek Anthology 7.407

Sappho was the first to leap from the prominent rock
in her amorous pursuit of the proud Phaon.
But now by my vow I shall praise your sacred
precinct on the Leukadian Cliff, O Lord Apollo.

Menandros, quoted in Strabon Geography 10.452

Some say there are nine Muses. Count again.
    Behold the tenth: Sappho of Lesbos.

Plato, in The Greek Anthology 9.506

Stranger, if you sail to Mytilini, city of beautiful dances
    that kindled the fire of Sappho's beauty . . .

Nossis, in The Greek Anthology 7.718

And you know how the Lesbian Alkaios played
many songs on the lyre about his warm love
for Sappho. He was a poet who loved Sappho,
the nightingale of song, but he annoyed Anakreon,
poet of Teos, because of his eloquence.

Hermesianax, in Athinaios Scholars at Dinner 598B

Learn the birthplace and ancestry
of the foremost nine lyric poets; observe
their fathers and dialects.
First was Alkaios from Mytilini,
the honored musical son of Aiolos.
After him, from the same land
and dialect, came the daughter
of Kleis and Ierigyios: Sappho.

Scholiast on Pindar 1.10

Portrait of Sappho

Painter, creative Nature herself gave you the Pierian
Muse from Mytilini to portray. Clarity is in her eyes
and this plainly reveals an imagination full of
    intelligence.
Her flesh is smooth and not painted unnaturally,
showing her simplicity. Mingled in her face are joy
and intellectual spirit, of the Muse joined with Kypris.

Damohares, in *The Greek Anthology* 16.310

Sappho's kisses would be sweet; sweet the embraces
of her snowy thighs and sweet all her body.
But her soul is adamantly unyielding. For her love stops
at her lips and the rest she keeps virgin.
Who can suffer this? One who can stand this,
could easily endure the thirst of Tantalos.

Paulus Silentiarius, in *The Greek Anthology* 5.246

Among Lesbian women with lovely locks of hair,
    Sappho is the jewel.

Antipatros of Thessaloniki, in *The Greek Anthology* 9.26

Fate granted you no small glory
on the day you first saw the light
of the sun, Sappho, for we Muses
agreed that your words should be
deathless; and the Father of All,
the Thunderer, also concurred.
You will be sung by all mortal men,
and not be poor in glorious fame.

Anonymous, in The Greek Anthology 9.521

Sappho was not ninth among men
but rather tenth among the lovely Muses.

Anonymous, in The Greek Anthology 9.571

Come to the shimmering precinct of bull-faced Hera,
   women of Lesbos, your delicate feet
spinning as you dance beautifully for the goddess.
   Sappho will lead, her golden lyre
in her hand. You radiate as you dance. You seem
   to hear Kalliopi's thrilling song.

Anonymous, in The Greek Anthology 9.189

From Latin Poetry on Sappho

The love still breathes, the flame is still alive
that the Aiolian woman girl sang to her lyre.

Horace Odes 4.9.11

The manly Sappho tames the muse of Archilochos
   through her prosody . . .

Horace Epode 1.19.28

A girl more refined than the Sapphic Muse.

Catullus 35.16

What did Sappho of Lesbos teach
   but how to love women?

Ovid *Tristia* 2.363

Sappho sang:
   In those days when Atthis was small
   my own girlhood was blossoming.

Terentianus Maurus *On Meters* 6

Sappho to Phaon

Say, lovely youth that dost my heart command,
Can Phaon's eyes forget his Sappho's hand?
Must then her name the wretched writer prove,
To thy remembrance lost as to thy love?

Ask not the cause that I new numbers choose,
The lute neglected and the lyric Muse:
Love taught my tears in sadder notes to flow,
And tuned my heart to elegies of woe.
I burn, I burn, as when through ripened corn
By driving winds the spreading flames are borne.
Phaon to Aetna's scorching fields retires,
While I consume with more than Aetna's fires.
No more my soul a charm in music finds;
Music has charms alone for peaceful minds:
Soft scenes of solitude no more can please;
Love enters there and I'm my own disease.
No more the Lesbian dames my passion move,
Once the dear objects of my guilty love:
All other loves are lost in only thine,

Testimonia and Encomia   232

Ah, youth ungrateful to a flame like mine!
Whom would not all those blooming charms surprise,
Those heavenly looks and dear deluding eyes?
The harp and bow would you like Phoebus bear,
A brighter Phoebus Phaon might appear:
Would you with ivy wreathe your flowing hair,
Not Bacchus' self with Phaon could compare:
Yet Phoebus loved, and Bacchus felt the flame;
One Daphne warmed and one the Cretan dame;
Nymphs that in verse no more could rival me
Than e'en those gods contend in charms with thee.
The Muses teach me all their softest lays,
And the wide world resounds with Sappho's praise.
Though great Alcaeus more sublimely sings
And strikes with bolder rage the sounding strings,
No less renown attends the moving lyre
Which Venus tunes and all her Loves inspire.
To me what Nature has in charms denied
Is well by wit's more lasting flames supplied.
Though short my stature, yet my name extends
To heaven itself and earth's remotest ends:
Brown as I am, an Aithiopian dame
Inspired young Perseus with a generous flame:
Turtles and doves of different hue unite,
And glossy jet is paired with shining white.
If to no charms thou wilt thy heart resign
But such as merit, such as equal thine,
By none, alas, by none thou canst be moved;
Phaon alone by Phaon must be loved.
Yet once thy Sappho could thy cares employ;
Once in her arms you centred all your joy:
No time the dear remembrance can remove,
For oh how vast a memory has love!
My music then you could for ever hear,

And all my words were music to your ear:
You stopt with kisses my enchanting tongue,
And found my kisses sweeter than my song.
In all I pleased, but most in what was best;
And the last joy was dearer than the rest:
Then with each word, each glance, each motion fired
You still enjoyed, and yet you still desired,
Till all dissolving in the trance we lay
And in tumultuous raptures died away.

The fair Sicilians now thy soul inflame:
Why was I born, ye gods, a Lesbian dame?
But ah, beware, Sicilian nymphs, nor boast
That wandering heart which I so lately lost;
Nor be with all those tempting words abused:
Those tempting words were all to Sappho used.
And you that rule Sicilia's happy plains,
Have pity, Venus, on your poet's pains.

Shall fortune still in one sad tenor run
And still increase the woes so soon begun?
Inured to sorrow from my tender years,
My parent's ashes drank my early tears:
My brother next, neglecting wealth and fame,
Ignobly burned in a destructive flame:
An infant daughter late my griefs increased,
And all a mother's cares distract my breast.
Alas, what more could Fate itself impose,
But thee, the last and greatest of my woes?
No more my robes in waving purple flow,
Nor on my hand the sparkling diamonds glow;
No more my locks in ringlets curled diffuse
The costly sweetness of Arabian dews;
Nor braids of gold the varied tresses bind

That fly disordered with the wanton wind.
For whom should Sappho use such arts as these?
He's gone whom only she desired to please!
Cupid's light darts my tender bosom move;
Still is there cause for Sappho still to love;
So from my birth the Sisters fixed my doom,
And gave to Venus all my life to come;
Or, while my Muse in melting notes complains,
My yielding heart keeps measure to my strains.
By charms like thine, which all my soul have won,
Who might not—ah, who would not be undone?
For those, Aurora Cephalus might scorn,
And with fresh blushes paint the conscious morn:
For those, might Cynthia lengthen Phaon's sleep,
And bid Endymion nightly tend his sheep:
Venus for those had rapt thee to the skies,
But Mars on thee might look with Venus' eyes.
O scarce a youth, yet scarce a tender boy!
O useful time for lovers to employ!
Pride of thy age, and glory of thy race,
Come to these arms and melt in this embrace!
The vows you never will return, receive;
And take at least the love you will not give.
See, while I write, my words are lost in tears:
The less my sense, the more my love appears.

Sure 'twas not much to bid one kind adieu:
At least, to feign was never hard to you.
"Farewell, my Lesbian love," you might have said;
Or coldly thus, "Farewell, O Lesbian maid."
No tear did you, no parting kiss receive,
Nor knew I then how much I was to grieve.
No lover's gift your Sappho could confer;

And wrongs and woes were all you left with her.
No charge I gave you, and no charge could give
But this,—"Be mindful of our loves, and live."
Now by the Nine, those powers adored by me,
And Love, the god that ever waits on thee;—
When first I heard (from whom I hardly knew)
That you were fled, and all my joys with you,
Like some sad statue, speechless, pale I stood;
Grief chilled my breast and stopt my freezing blood;
No sigh to rise, no tear had power to flow,
Fixed in a stupid lethargy of woe.
But when its way the impetuous passion found,
I rend my tresses and my breast I wound;
I rave, then weep; I curse, and then complain;
Now swell to rage, now melt in tears again.
Not fiercer pangs distract the mournful dame
Whose first-born infant feeds the funeral flame.
My scornful brother with a smile appears,
Insults my woes, and triumphs in my tears;
His hated image ever haunts my eyes;—
"And why this grief? thy daughter lives," he cries.
Stung with my love and furious with despair,
All torn my garments and my bosom bare,
My woes, thy crimes, I to the world proclaim;
Such inconsistent things are love and shame.
Tis thou art all my care and my delight,
My daily longing and my dream by night.—
O night more pleasing than the brightest day,
When fancy gives what absence takes away,
And, dressed in all its visionary charms,
Restores my fair deserter to my arms.
Then round your neck in wanton wreath I twine;
Then you, methinks, as fondly circle mine:

A thousand tender words I hear and speak;
A thousand melting kisses give and take:
Then fiercer joys; I blush to mention these,
Yet, while I blush, confess how much they please.
But when with day the sweet delusions fly,
And all things wake to life and joy, but I;
As if once more forsaken, I complain,
And close my eyes to dream of you again:
Then frantic rise; and, like some fury, rove
Through lonely plains, and through the silent grove,
As if the silent grove and lonely plains,
That knew my pleasures, could relieve my pains.
I view the grotto, once the scene of love,
The rocks around, the hanging roofs above,
That charmed me more, with native moss o'ergrown,
Than Phrygian marble or the Parian stone:
I find the shades that veiled our joys before;
But, Phaon gone, those shades delight no more.
Here the pressed herbs with bending tops betray
Where oft entwined in amorous folds we lay;
I kiss that earth which once was pressed by you,
And all with tears the withering herbs bedew.
For thee the fading trees appear to mourn,
And birds defer their songs till thy return:
Night shades the groves, and all in silence lie,—
All but the mournful Philomel and I:
With mournful Philomel I join my strain;
Of Jereus she, of Phaon I complain.

A spring there is whose silver waters show,
Clear as a glass, the shining sands below:
A flowery lotos spreads its arms above,
Shades all the banks and seems itself a grove;

Eternal greens the mossy margin grace,
Watched by the sylvan genius of the place:
Here as I lay, and swelled with tears the flood,
Before my sight a watery virgin stood:
She stood and cried,—"O you that love in vain,
Fly hence and seek the fair Leucadian main:
There stands a rock from whose impending steep
Apollo's fane surveys the rolling deep;
There injured lovers, leaping from above,
Their flames extinguish and forget to love.
Deucalion once with hopeless fury burned;
In vain he loved, relentless Pyrrha scorned.
But when from hence he plunged into the main
Deucalion scorned, and Pyrrha loved in vain.
Haste, Sappho, haste, from high Leucadia throw
Thy wretched weight, nor dread the deeps below."

She spoke, and vanished with the voice: I rise,
And silent tears fall trickling from my eyes.
I go, ye nymphs, those rocks and seas to prove:
How much I fear, but ah, how much I love!
I go, ye nymphs, where furious love inspires;
Let female fears submit to female fires:
To rocks and seas I fly from Phaon's hate,
And hope from seas and rocks a milder fate.
Ye gentle gales, beneath my body blow,
And softly lay me on the waves below.
And thou, kind Love, my sinking limbs sustain,
Spread thy soft wings and waft me o'er the main,
Nor let a lover's death the guiltless flood profane.
On Phoebus' shrine my harp I'll then bestow,
And this inscription shall be placed below:—
"Here she who sung, to him that did inspire,
Sappho to Phoebus consecrates her lyre:

What suits with Sappho, Phoebus, suits with thee;
The gift, the giver, and the god agree."

But why, alas, relentless youth, ah, why
To distant seas must tender Sappho fly?
Thy charms than those may far more powerful be,
And Phoebus' self is less a god to me.
Ah, canst thou doom me to the rocks and sea,
O far more faithless and more hard than they?
Ah, canst thou rather see this tender breast
Dashed on these rocks than to thy bosom pressed?
This breast, which once, in vain! you liked so well;
Where the Loves played, and where the Muses dwell.
Alas, the Muses now no more inspire;
Untuned my lute, and silent is my lyre:
My languid numbers have forgot to flow,
And fancy sinks beneath the weight of woe.

Ye Lesbian virgins and ye Lesbian dames,
Themes of my verse and objects of my flames,
No more your groves with my glad songs shall ring;
No more these hands shall touch the trembling string:
My Phaon's fled, and I those arts resign:
(Wretch that I am, to call that Phaon mine!)
Return, fair youth, return, and bring along
Joy to my soul and vigour to my song.
Absent from thee, the poet's flame expires;
But ah, how fiercely burn the lover's fires!
Gods, can no prayers, no signs, no numbers move
One savage heart, or teach it how to love?
The winds my prayers, my sighs, my numbers bear;
The flying winds have lost them all in air.
Or when, alas, shall more auspicious gales
To these fond eyes restore thy welcome sails?
If you return, ah, why these long delays?

Poor Sappho dies while careless Phaon stays.
O launch the bark, nor fear the watery plain:
Venus for thee shall smoothe her native main.
O launch thy bark, secure of prosperous gales:
Cupid for thee shall spread the swelling sails.
If you will fly—(yet ah, what cause can be,
Too cruel youth, that you should fly from me?)
If not from Phaon I must hope for ease,
Ah, let me seek it from the raging seas;
To raging seas unpitied I'll remove;
And either cease to live or cease to love.

Ovid "Heroic Epistle, XV"
translated by Alexander Pope, 1707

Modern Literature*

After dark vapours have oppressed our plains

After dark vapours have oppressed our plains
   For a long dreary season, comes a day
   Born of the gentle South, and clears away
From the sick heavens all unseemly stains.
The anxious month, relieving from its pains,
   Takes as a long-lost right the feel of May,
   The eyelids with the passing coolness play,
Like rose leaves with the drip of summer rains.
And calmest thoughts come round us as of leaves
   Budding—fruit ripening in the stillness—autumn suns
Smiling at eve upon the quiet sheaves—

---

* In addition to ancient testimonia, abundant praise and reference to Sappho in literature continues into modern times, and especially since the nineteenth century. Most of it is not worthy of Sappho, but included here are a few outstanding ones by major poets.

Sweet Sappho's cheek—a sleeping infant's breath—
   The gradual sand through an hour-glass runs—
A woodland rivulet—a Poet's death.

John Keats (1795–1821)

Damned Women

Like pensive cattle lying on the sand,
They turn their eyes to the sea's horizon,
Their feet and hands creeping slowly to band
And fuse in soft tremors and bitter abandon.

Some of these hearts beguiled by secrets shared
Deep in the woods where brooks chat noisily
Spell out their furtive love as children carve
Initials on green bark of a young tree.

Others are walking slow and grave like nuns
Across the rock fields filled with apparitions
Where once Saint Anthony saw lava stun
And surge like nude blue breasts of his temptation.

And some by torchlight of quiescent caves,
A resin smell in the old Pagan shrine,
Call for your help, Bacchus, healer who saves
And relieves them from screaming heat and pain,

Others wear scapulars round their throat,
Hiding a whip under their draping skirt,
And in dark forests and lonely night
Combine the foam of bliss with tearful hurt.

O virgins, demons, O monsters, martyrs,
Great spirits pondering reality,
Seeking the infinite, saints and satyrs,
Racked with sobs, breaking in ecstasy,

You whom my soul has followed to your hell,
Poor sisters, I love and pity you for your part
For desolate grief, for thirst your citadel,
And urns of love filling your great hearts.

Charles Baudelaire (1821–1867)
Translated by Willis Barnstone

Ιμέρρω
Thy soul
Grown delicate with satieties,
Atthis.
O Atthis,
I long for thy lips.
I long for thy narrow breasts,
Thou restless, ungathered.

Ezra Pound, 1917

A Shower

That sputter of rain, flipping the hedge rows
And making the highways hiss,
How I love it!
And the touch of you upon my arm
As you press against me that my umbrella
May cover you.
Tinkle of drops on stretched silk.
We murmur through green branches.

Amy Lowell, 1919

Taking us by and large, we're a queer lot
We women who write poetry. And when you think
How few of us they've been, it's queerer still . . .

There's Sapho, now I wonder what was Sapho.
I know a single slender thing about her:
That, loving, she was like a burning birch-tree
All tall and glittering fire, and that she wrote
Like the same fire caught up to Heaven and held there
And she is Sapho — Sapho — not Miss or Mrs,
A leaping fire we call so for convenience . . .

Amy Lowell, from "What O'Clock?," 1925

THREE POEMS FROM NEW POEMS (NEUE GEDICHTE) BY RAINER MARIA RILKE*

Eranna to Sappho

You the wild far-hurling woman
like a spear among common things,
I lay with my sisters. Your song burst
cast me somewhere. I don't know where I am.
No one can bring me back.

My sisters think of me and weave,
and in my house familiar steps.
Only I am far off and given away
and tremble like a plea.
The beauty goddess burns in her myths
and lives my life.

Sappho to Eranna

I want to crush your heart,
I want to sword you with an ivy-wreathed staff.
Like dying I want to pierce you

---

* All three selections are translated by Willis Barnstone.

and, like the grave, in all these things
I want to pass you on

Sappho to Alkaios (fragment)

And what else can you say to me,
and what do you have to do with my soul
when you avoid me, lowering your eyes
before what you won't reveal? Sir,

take a look. Our rapture is saying
these things; it sweeps us into fame.
Thinking of it I tell you: under you
our sweet virginity perished,

and I know and those who know me
know that mine, guarded by the god,
was unstained while Mitylini
like an apple orchard at night

grew fragrant with our ripening breasts.
Yes, these breasts, which you didn't choose
like someone collecting wreaths of fruit
since you as lover turned your face away.
Go. Leave me. What you withhold
may then be heard in my lyre, in equipoise.
This god is of no help to a couple,
but when he penetrates one . . .

EPILOGUE

by William E. McCulloh, Kenyon College

How MANY READERS of this book recall when they first heard of Sappho?* My earliest recollection is the sight of her name in a footnote to *The Waste Land*, but there must have been earlier occasions, since I already knew she was a famed poet. Why was she famous? It took time for me to understand that.

The first glimpse of her poetry came in college, through the Latin mirror of Catullus 51 (see note for fragment 31 in the Sources), when I looked with dim comprehension at the Greek original below it in the editor's note. Only in graduate school did my direct acquaintance properly begin. I memorized poem 1 (until last year, the only surviving complete poem) and reached out from there toward any of the fragments that shone brightly to me in my still benighted condition.[†]

Beyond this direct encounter, my understanding of what Sappho means for poetry and humanity has advanced by fits and starts, which were also a series of gifts. The first was the great gift of working with Willis Barnstone long ago on Greek lyric poetry, including his earlier translation of Sappho.

---

* On Lesbos the name was pronounced roughly like *Psappo*.

† Thirty years later, when I recited poem 1 from memory at a *glendi* on Kalymnos, the grizzled *tsambouna* player kept muttering, "I don't understand a word of it."

Then came the bounty of reading with my students not only Sappho but also those Sapphic legatees Plato and Longus (whose *Daphnis and Chloë* is now widely recognized as a masterpiece). Then—and it will seem puzzling until the end of this Epilogue—Pseudo-Dionysios the Areopagite, who infused Platonism into the mystical theology of Europe.

And now a final gift again from Willis: the reading of Sappho more fully and closely than ever before.* All of these benefactions have helped me to see more fully what Sappho has wrought. Let me briefly traverse a path into the Sapphic realm, starting (as one should) from what is immediately before me—the very texture of her song:

"The euphony and charm of this passage [poem 1, "Prayer to Afroditi"] lie in the cohesion and smoothness of the joinery. Words are juxtaposed and interwoven according to certain natural affinities and groupings of the letters." (Dionysios of Halikarnassos, translated in Campbell 1988, 55) Sappho sings herself into our ears and our hearts even without her melodies. The euphony praised by Dionysios rides on her rhythms, even in many of her most pathetic fragments:

> glukea mater otoi dunamai kreken ton iston u_u_u_ _|
> uu_u_u_ _ (92, "Paralysis"— pronounce with Continental vowels)

> kai potheo kai maomai _u_ _ _uu_ (36, "Absence")

> mete moi meli mete melissa _u_uu_uu_ _ (146, "Choosing")

No translation can catch her rhythms for long without losing her directness, vividness, and concision, though some have tried hard (Richmond Lattimore sometimes came close). Others have

---

* I am grateful also to my friend Andrew Duffy for electronic help with the Greek text.

ventured instead to use her meters—especially her stanza—in their own fresh creations.

Catullus and Horace are the greatest of these, but even in English we have, for example, Tennyson, Swinburne, Symonds, and Pound. Here is Swinburne:

> ... and I too,

> Full of the vision,

> Saw the white implacable Aphrodite,
> Saw the hair unbound and the feet unsandalled
> Shine as fire of sunset on western waters;
> Saw the reluctant

> Feet, the straining plumes of the doves that drew her,
> Looking always, looking with necks reverted,
> Back to Lesbos, back to the hills whereunder
> Shone Mitylene ...

> (from "Sapphics")

Sappho calls upon her Muses, her music, to sing beauty and Eros above all. She is the first poet to place these powers at the center of song and life. Two of her many later admirers caught up her song in special ways that ever after have echoed—often unrecognized or unacknowledged—in philosophy and poetry:

Shelley said, "Plato was essentially a poet: the truth and splendor of his imagery and the melody of his language are the most intense that it is possible to conceive" ("A Defence of Poetry"). *Symposium* and *Phaedrus* in the music of prose sing a vision of beauty and Eros at the heart of all reality. (Aristotle, Plato's pupil, says of the Prime Mover, "It moves [the stars] as their beloved.")

And Longus in the musical prose of *Daphnis and Chloë* tells us:

> . . . no one has escaped Eros, nor shall, as long as
> beauty exists and eyes see. . . . He has more power
> than even Zeus. He rules the elements, rules the
> stars, rules the gods. . . . All flowers are the work of
> Eros, all trees are his creations. Through him the
> rivers flow and the winds blow. (Prologue, and
> Book II.7)

Already (thanks to the mysterious intervention of the Areopagite, who teaches that ecstatic Eros and beauty are at the heart of Divinity Itself, so far as we may know and speak thereof—but that is another story) we are not far from Dante and "the Love that moves the sun and other stars." Willis Barnstone with his direct, vivid, concise translation returns us anew to the voice that began this great song:

> . . . Eros has got me
> brightness and the beauty of the sun.

SOURCES, NOTES, AND COMMENTARY

IN THIS SECTION, I provide source and additional information for the poems translated in this edition, as well as ancient commentary related to the poems. The notes that follow give, first, the source of the poem, then any ancient commentary in quotation marks, followed by my own explanatory comments. For more information on the sources, see the Introduction. More information on the poems is also provided in the Glossary.

1 *Papyri Oxyrhynchus* 2288. Also Dionysios of Halikarnassos *On Literary Composition* 23 (6.114ss Usener-Radermacher).

"I shall now give paradigms of this style (that is, polished and exuberant), selecting Sappho among poets and Isokratis among orators. I begin with the lyric poet." [There follows the poem, and then again Dionysios.] "The euphony and charm of this passage lie in the cohesion and smoothness of the connecting phrases. For the words are juxtaposed and interwoven according to the natural affinities and groupings of the letters. . . ." See the Testimonia for a more complete context of the poem, being with "The polished and florid composition . . ."

This poem to Afroditi is usually considered one of two complete poems of Sappho that have survived. Though it is therefore not a fragment, by accepted convention all lines of Sappho are identified by their "fragment" number, and here too we refer to it as fragment 1. The other complete poem, fragment 58, was published for the first time in 2005. There are fragments of other poems, however, that have more lines than this complete poem, such as fragment 44, "Wedding of Andromache and Hektor."

Despite the tone of intimate friendship and cheerful camaraderie, the poem to Afroditi has the formal structure of a prayer, with the expected invocation, sanction, and entreaty.

2 *Ostracon Florentinum*, ed. M. Norsa, Annali della reale Scuola normale superiore di Pisa, Lettere, Storia e Filosofia, series 2, 6 (1937).

Kriti [Crete] was thought to be the original seat of worship of Afroditi, or so its inhabitants claimed. The scene described here is a real place in Lesbos, devoted to the worship of Afroditi. Apples and horses were symbols of Afroditi, who was known as Afroditi of the Apples as well as Afroditi of the Horses. The prayer for epiphany in the poem is by no means proof that Sappho was a priestess or a poet of cult songs. Her concern with Afroditi was with a figure who represented beauty and love.

Line 11 retains only the first two words, and line 12 is missing altogether. The English translation might retain obediently, not indent, line 11 and leave an extra blank line or brackets between the third and fourth stanzas. However, here as elsewhere I attempt to go partway in reflecting the abused Greek text (which can have its own delight and freshness in mirrored English). Normally I limit the mirror so the English can live. But sometimes in treating very brief fragments, I try to make the English wording correspond in spacing as closely as possible. This device may still make the English conversion intelligible while giving it an interesting form based on the haphazard remains of the Greek text.

Fragment 2 is preceded on the same *Ostracon Florentinum* (an ostracon is a potsherd—a fragment of broken pottery) by the fragmentary phrase ρανοθεν κατιου. This can plausibly be restored to mean "coming down from heaven." It might or might not have directly preceded fragment 2 itself.

3 *Papyri Berlin* 5006 + *Papyri Oxyrhynchus* 3.424.6–18.

This important text is a botched column, yet remarkable in its power. For some broken words, I have followed the guesses of several scholars, especially Max Treu, who goes further in his German translation to make sense. He places conjectures for half words in brackets. I have made guesses for a few words here, too, though elsewhere I avoid the significant guesses outside of the endnotes.

4 *Papyri Berlin* 5006.

The text is obviously fragmentary, scarcely more than a column of words, yet the words are intelligible; the syntax and connective words present the main difficulty. Ezra Pound's early poem imitating Sappho suggests a similar scrap of papyrus:

> *Papyrus*
>
> Spring . . .
> Too long . . .
> Gongula . . .

5 *Papyri Oxyrhynchus* 7 + 2289.6.

Nereids are sea nymphs or mermaids.

The poem is to Sappho's brother Haraxos. The black torment is presumably his Egyptian mistress, Doriha, on whom Haraxos was "wasting" his fortune. In the mutilated lines that follow (not included here), Sappho seems to broaden her attack on Doriha. There are numerous attack poems against Doriha, or Rodopis, which are found much later in Herodotos and Strabon and in Athinaios's *Scholars at Dinner.* This woman who is the object of Sappho's hostilities was a Thracian by birth, who later went to Egypt as a prostitute. She became the mistress of Sappho's brother Haraxos, who imported Lesbian wine to Naukratis. Sappho attacks her in several poems, presumably because Doriha captivated her brother and swindled him in commerce. Sappho wants his attention, and for him to reform and come back. For more, see the Testimonia, and Lobel and Page (202) for the traditional poems against Doriha.

5a, b, c incert. Herodianos *On Anomalous Words* 26 (ii 932 Lentz).

The translation of 5b and c is uncertain, but they are fascinating and so I include them, following David Campbell's guesses, and repeating his apology about the elusive meaning.

6 *Papyri Oxyrhynchus* 2289 frag. 1 a, b.

7 *Papyri Oxyrhynchus* 2289 frag. 2.

9 *Papyri Oxyrhynchus* 2289 frag. 4.
Another talk with Hera.

15 *Papyri Oxyrhynchus* 1231 frag. 1 col. 1.1–12 + frag. 3.
After "Blessed," the goddess's name has not survived. Sappho was addressing, here as elsewhere, Afroditi.

16 *Papyri Oxyrhynchus* 1231 frag. 1 col. 1.13–34, col. 2.1 + 2166(a) 2 (*Ox. Pap.* 21, p. 122) + P.S.I. 123.1–2.
Sappho begins the poem with a paratactic trope, found also in Tyrtaios's famous poem on the Spartan soldier, fragment 9, and Pindar *Olympian Odes* 1, to compare the apparent splendor of military spectacles with the power of love. While she does not dull the public sparkle of the masculine world of war, to her all of this bright clutter of history cannot match the illumination of love and physical beauty in her personal world. While Sappho writes at least once in a Homeric voice, speaking of the wedding of Andromache and Hektor in fragment 44, she has chosen in that poem to celebrate the wedding of these two people, who are perhaps the two most developed and sympathetic characters in the *Iliad*, rather than to celebrate a warring hero. She also appears to show a preference for the Trojans over the Achaians (the Greeks), which may also be Homer's preference, as he finishes his epic with great sympathy for the fallen Hektor, his funeral, the bereaved Andromache, and the soon-to-be annihilated Trojans. So after stating how once the gaze of love and powers of Afroditi led Helen to choose her lover before family, at whatever cost, Sappho reaffirms the centrality of love by comparing chronicle event to personal circumstance. Sappho would rather gaze at her beloved than to behold all the shining hoplites (foot soldiers) and chariots in Lydia.

16 incert. Hefaistion *Handbook of Meters* 11.3, 5 (pp. 35–36 Consbruch).

"The Aiolian composed acatalectic ionic a maiore trimeters in two ways, from two ionics and a trochaic metrical foot, [verse follows] and others from one ionic and two trochaic metrical feet. In their tetrameters they sometimes begin with a short syllable as in their trimeters [verse follows]."

The poem is attributed to Sappho or Alkaios but clearly appears to be Sappho's. It is similar in tone to fragment 154, with lines about women before an altar in Kriti, and to "Afroditi of the Flowers at Knossos" (fragment 2).

17 *P.S.I.* 2.123.3–12 + *Papyri Oxyrhynchus* 1231 frag. 1 col. 2.2–21 + 2166a + *Papyri Oxyrhynchus* 2289 frag. 9.

18 *Papyri Oxyrhynchus* 1231 frag. 1 col. 2.22–27 (vi versuum initia).

18b, c incert. *Papyri Oxyrhynchus* 220 col 9.7ss (Heph. p. 405 Consbruch).

19 *Papyri Oxyrhynchus* 1231 frag. 2.

20 *Papyri Oxyrhynchus* 2131 frag. 9 + 2166(a)4a (*Ox. Pap.* 21, p. 122) (xxiv versuum frr.).

The text is very fragmentary. David A. Campbell's literal translation in volume one of *Greek Lyric* reads: ". . . brightness . . . with the help of good fortune . . . to gain (the harbour?) . . . beach (earth?) . . . the sailors (are unwilling?) . . . great gusts . . . and on dry land . . . sail . . . the cargo . . . since . . . flowing (?) many . . . (receive?) . . . tasks . . . dry land . . ." "To Lady Hera" (fragment 17), as well as the other poems in this section, is a poem related to shrines and goddesses. Sappho addresses many gods in her poems, but when asking for help from a friendly deity, she normally addresses a goddess. As can be seen, the poem is from a strip of papyrus. The poem is one that has the sea-storm qualities of Alkaios, but here there is less heroic symbolism and actual personal and immediate speech. It gives a hint of the broadness of Sappho's vision and themes that were surely developed in other lost poems.

21 *Papyri Oxyrhynchus* 1231 frag. 10.
The text is very fragmentary. David A. Campbell's translation in the first volume of *Greek Lyric* reads: "...(in possession of?)...pity...trembling...old age now...(my) sky...covers...(Love?) flies pursuing (the young?)...glorious...taking (your lyre?) sing to us of the violet-robed one...especially wanders..."

22 *Papyri Oxyrhynchus* 1231 frag. 12, 15.

23 *Papyri Oxyrhynchus,* 1231 frag. 14.
Hermioni (Hermione) was Helen's daughter.

24a, b, c
24a: *Papyri Oxyrhynchus* 1231 frag. 13 + 2166(a)7a (*Ox. Pap.* 21, p. 124); 24b: *Ox. Pap.* 1231 frag. 17; 24c: *Ox. Pap.* 1231 frag. 22 + 25.
These wonderful fragments have the nostalgia of Constantine Cavafy's many memory poems, where youth is contrasted with the harshness of age.

25 incert. 1.55b (p. 50s Wendel).
This line is attributed to Sappho or Alkaios, but it is surely by Sappho.

26 *Papyri Oxyrhynchus* 1231, frag. 16.

27 *Papyri Oxyrhynchus* 1231 frag. 50–54 + 2166(a)5 (*Ox. Pap.* 21, p. 123).

27 incert. Papyrus fragment 2977a (ed. Oellacher, M.P.E. R., n.s., Pt. 1 p. 88) fr. 1(a).
Menelaos can also be rendered "Meneleos."

30 *Papyri Oxyrhynchus* 1231 frag. 56 + 2166(a)6a.

This song sung by girls outside the window of the newlyweds humorously tells the groom to awaken and go out and join his old friends. The taunting tone goes well with the happiness of the occasion.

31 Longinos *On the Sublime* 10.1–3.

We owe the preservation of fragment 31 to the major Alexandrian literary critic Longinos, who cited these lines as an example of the sublime and the ecstatic. Fragment 31 is probably the most frequently translated of Sappho's poems, from Catullus to William Carlos Williams. Catullus's fifty-first ode to Lesbia—"referring to Sappho but actually addressed to his lover Clodia. It is a close version of Sappho's poem, and a precious document and major poem:

> *Ille mi par esse deo videtur,*
> *ille, si fas est, superare divos,*
> *qui sedens adversus identidem te*
>   *spectat et audit*
>
> *dulce ridentem, misero quod omnis*
> *scripit sensus mihi: nam simul te,*
>   *Lesbia, aspexi, nihil est super mi*
>
> *lingua sed torpet, tenuis sub artus*
> *flamma demanat, sonitu suopte*
> *tintinant aures, gemina teguntur*
>   *lumina nocte.*
>
> *otium, Catulle, tibi molestum est:*
> *otio exsultas nimiumque gestis:*
> *otium et reges prius et beatas*
>   *perdidit urbes.*

> To me that man seems like a god,
> greater than a god, if that can be,
> who sitting beside you steadily
>   watches you,

hearing your soft laughter that rips
my senses away, hopeless, for as soon
as I gaze at you, Lesbia, nothing is left
   of me,

my tongue is broken, a thin fire
spreads through my limbs, my ears ring
inside, and my eyes are covered
   in darkness!

but Catullus your laziness hurts you,
you exult in laziness and lust.
In old times sloth has ruined kings
   and rich cities.

A recent tradition of scholarship holds Sappho's poem to be a
wedding song to be sung before a bride and groom. There is no
internal evidence of this, and these verses of violent personal pas-
sion would be inappropriate at the ceremony. The poem is a mar-
vel of candor and power in which Sappho states her hurt before
the calm godlike man and describes with striking objectivity and
detachment the physical symptoms of her passionate love for the
girl. A few decades earlier, Archilochos, the first poet to speak of
the passions of the outsider and individual, had written:

I lie here miserable and broken with desire,
pierced through to the bones by the bitterness
of this god-given painful love.
O comrade, this passion makes my limbs limp
and tramples over me. (frag. 104 Diehl.)*

32 Apollonios Dyskolos *Pronouns* 144a (1.113 Schneider).
   "Aiolic has the forms ἀμμέτερος and ἄμμος for 'our,' ὔμμος
for 'your,' and σφός for 'their.' See Sappho: [verse follows]."
   Literally, "giving their works."

* Willis Barnstone, trans., *Sappho and the Greek Lyric Poets* (New York:
Schocken Books, 1987, p. 33).

33 Apollonios Dyskolos *Syntax* 3.247 (2.350 Uhlig).
The grammarian Apollonios Dyskolos writes, "There are the adverbs that indicate prayer as αἴθε: [verse follows]."

34 Eustathios 729.21, on the *Iliad* 8.555.
The grammarian Eustathios writes: "In the expression 'around the shining moon,' one should not interpret this as the full moon, for then the stars are dim because they are outshone, for as Sappho says somewhere: [verse follows]."
Probably Sappho's lines refer to the notion that one of her companions outshone all the others in beauty. As Ann Carson and others note, the Roman emperor Julian writes in a letter to his instructor the sophist Hekebolios: "Sappho says the moon is silver and so conceals all other stars from view" (*Letters*, 387a).

36 *Etymologicum Genuinum* (p. 31 Calame) = *Etymologicum Magnum* 485.41.
"The Aiolic writers use ποθήω for ποθέω, 'I long for.'"
These five words in Greek crystallize one essential mood of Sappho.

37 *Etymologicum Genuinum* (p. 36 Calame) = *Etymologicum Magnum* 576.23ss.
"It is noted that Aiolic writers call σταλαγμός [pain] 'a dripping,' as if a pain 'wounds.' For in Aiolic σσ is changed to ζ. ἐπιπλήσσω becomes ἐπιπλαζω. [Verse follows.]"

38 Apollonios Dyskolos *Pronouns* 127a (1100 Schneider).
Aiolic writers use ἄμμε, "us." While "you burn us" is a close translation of the Greek, some scholars argue that instead of "us," the singular pronoun "me" is intended. See Anne Carson, *If Not Winter: Fragments of Sappho* (New York: Vintage Books, 2002), pp. 365–66, for her elaboration of the pronoun usage and the entire sentence.

39 Scholiast on Aristophanes' *Peace* 1174 (p. 205 Dübner).
"For the Lydian dyes differ . . . and Sappho says: [lines follow]."
Pollux identifies Sappho's word with a type of sandal.

40 Apollonios Dyskolos *Pronouns* 104c (1.81 Schneider) + incert 13.
"σοί, 'to you,' the Attic form, is used also in Ionic and Aiolic.
See Sappho: [verses follow]."
Other texts give a sequel to the LP 40 fragment, so it would
read:

> I leave you
> the flesh of a white goat
> and will pour wine over it

The words refer to a sacrifice. Both lines are found in Apol-
lonios Dyskolos's *Pronouns* 104c. Here, as in Voigt, the first line,
40, and 40 incert. are gathered together. The extra line spacing
is to indicate that it is uncertain where in the original text that
line was.

41 Apollonios Dyskolos *Pronouns* 124c.
A comment on the Aiolic form of the pronoun "to you."

42 Scholiast on Pindar's *Pythian Odes* 1.0 (2.10 Drachmann).
The scholiast on Pindar writes: "Pindar has described a pic-
ture of an eagle perched on Zeus's scepter and lulled to sleep by
music, letting both wings lie still. . . . On the other hand Sappho
says of pigeons: [verse follows]."

43 *Papyri Oxyrhynchus* 1232 frag. 1 col. 1.5–9. Voigt is followed.
The reference is to a party or a night festival.

44 *Papyri Oxyrhynchus* 1232 frag. 1 col. 2–3, frag. 2 + m2076 col. 2.
Lobel and Page do not include this fragment. The poem ends
with "End of the Second Book of Sappho's Poems." This hymeneal
song, from the book of epithalamia, is more narratively epic and
Homeric in word and idea than any other existing fragment of

Sappho's. Because of these qualities not normally found in Sappho, Page casts some doubt as to her authorship. David A. Campbell and most scholars affirm her authorship. Campbell observes, "Sappho's authorship is confirmed by quotations in Athinaeus, Bekker's *Anecdota Graeca* and Ammonios." Here is another voice, a Homeric voice, which reveals her breadth.

Paean is *Paon* in Sappho's Aiolic Greek and is Apollo's title. In addition, the word *paean* can mean a joyful song or hymn of praise and thanksgiving.

44a Campbell = Alkaios 304 LP. *Papyri Fouad* 239.

This substantial fragment was copied in the second or third century C.E. and attributed to Alkaios, with uncertainty, by Lobel, and then by Lobel and Page. Other scholars assign it to Sappho. Max Treu made a strong and convincing case for Sappho's authorship in his *Sappho*. He cites the phrase "I shall always be a virgin" as Sappho's speech and rejects the Page argument. More recently Campbell includes it among Sappho's poems, while recognizing Lobel and Page's ascription to Alkaios. This poem, which has the élan and grandeur of Homer, adds a major woman deity to those whom Sappho admired. In its way it is a perfectly self-contained fragment, giving Artemis's origin, her own exuberant oath describing who she is, the name she has acquired among the gods and worshipers, and how in her life Artemis resisted the intrusions of Eros.

45 Apollonios Dyskolos *Pronouns* 119b (1.93 Schneider).

The grammarian Apollonios Dyskdolos says that Sappho spells the word ὑμεῖς, "you" (pl.) as ὔμμες in Aiolic.

46 Herodianos *On Anomalous Words* b39 (2.945 Lentz).

The comment concerns the word τύλη (cushion), that was not used by Attic writers but by Sappho in Book 2.

47 Maximus of Tyre *Orations* 18.9.

The rhetorician Maximus of Tyre writes, "Socrates says Eros is a sophist, Sappho calls him a weaver of tales. Eros makes Socrates mad for Phaidros, and Eros shook Sappho's heart like a wind felling an oak tree on a mountain."

48 Julian *Letter* 183 (p. 240s Bidez-Cumont).
In his letter to Iamblihus (who is actually dead by the time Julian writes him), Julian refers to these words by Sappho. His playful letter begins: "You came, yes, you came. Your letter came even though you were absent."

49 Hefaistion, *Handbook of Meters* 7.7 (p. 23 Consbruch).
"Among the types belonging to Aiolic dactylic verse, the pentameter is called the Sapphic 14-syllable, in which all of Sappho's *Book 2* is written: [line follows]."

Plutarch, 751d (4.343 Hubert).
In his *Dialogue on Love*, Plutarch puts the above line cited by Hefaistion together with a second line, which might, or more likely might not, have followed. Plutarch writes:
"Speaking to a girl who was still too young for marriage, Sappho says: [both lines of fragment follow]."

50 Galinos *Exhortation to Learning* 8.16s (1.113 Marquardt).
The author Galinos, who wrote on medicine, philosophy, and grammar, says of Sappho, "Since we know that the time of youth is like spring flowers and its pleasures do not last long, it is better to praise the Lesbian poet when she says: [verse follows]."

51 Hrysippos *On Negatives* 23 (*S.V.F.* 2.57 Arnim).
Sappho introduces a quandary with a negative, thereby affirming her uncertainty. Her tone is that of mischievous gravity.

52 Herodianos *On Anomalous Words* 7 (2.912 Lentz).
"Sappho [uses the form of ὄρανος, 'sky.']: [verse follows]."

53 Scholiast on Theokritos 28 arg. (p. 334 Wendel).
The cited line appears in a comment by the scholiast concerning Sappho's use of the sixteen-syllable meter in the Aiolic dialect.

54 Pollux *Vocabulary* 10.124 (2.227 Bethe).
The lexicographer Pollux writes: "It is said that Sappho was the first to use the word χλάμυν, 'mantle,' when she said of Eros [verse follows]."

55 Stobaios *Anthology* (*On Folly*) 3.4.12 (3.221ls Wachsmuth-Hense).
The fragment is from a poem in Stobaios's *Anthology* (*On Folly*), prefaced with the phrase "Sappho to a woman of no education." Plutarch says that the verse is addressed to a rich woman, but he also says to "an ignorant, uneducated woman."

56 Hrysippos *On Negatives* frag. 13 col. 8 (*S.V.F.* 2.55 Arnim).

57 Athinaios *Scholars at Dinner* 21bc (1.46 Kaibel).
"Sappho derides Andromeda in this way: [poem follows]." Fragment 57 is a good example where the source information yields essential information, which enters the title.

58b Campbell. 58b (lines 11–22) + Martin West (TLS 6.24.05).
The earlier segment of this poem was first published in 1922. All, or perhaps most of the rest of the poem was published in 2004 from a third-century B.C.E. papyrus found in the Cologne University archives. Martin. L. West first published the find in Greek in the *Zeitschrift für Papyrologie und Epigraphik* 151 (2005), 1–9, and in Greek along with his English translation in the *Times Literary Supplement*, June 21, 2005, 1.
The English translation here, by Willis Barnstone and William McCulloh, differs substantially from the version deciphered by Professor West. The appearance of this "second" complete

poem is a literary event, and, with the probability of more texts revealed through infra-ray technology, it is reasonable to believe that there will be more significant finds, through the spade and through improved reading technology of papyri and later parchments.

Dawn (Eos) carried off Tithonos, who was the brother of Priamos (Priam) and Dawn's lover. Dawn asked Zeus to make Tithonos immortal, but she forgot to ask also for the gift of eternal youth. Tithonos became older and older and began to shrink, though he had the range of her palace, and Dawn could hear his weak voice. When he could not walk she locked him in a chamber and eventually turned him into a grasshopper. Because Tithonos did not retain his youth, the mention of his name evokes a decrepit old man.

58c *Papyri Oxyrhynchus* 1787 frag. 1. 4–25, frag. 2.1 + frag. nov. (Lobel, 26).

Commenting on the last lines of the poem, Athinaios in *Scholars at Dinner* 15.687, writes: "So you think that refinement without virtue is desirable? But Sappho, who was a real woman and poet, was loath to separate good from refinement, saying, 'Yet I love refinement, and beauty and light are for me the same as desire for the sun.' It is therefore clear that the desire to live included for Sappho both the bright and the good, and these belong to virtue."

It is said that 58c may be from a separate poem or a part of 58b. However, 58c is contained as lines 25 and 26 in the earlier found *Oxyrhynchus* 1787 frag. 1. 4–25, frag. 2.1 + frag. nov. (Lobel Σ. μ.), which confirms that the lines were part of a major ancient papyrus containing Sappho's poems. However, since West's new 58b does not contain these in the text he has published, they make a fine sequel as a separate fragment. I should note that both Treu's and Campbell's guesses in their translations of 58 have proved to be remarkably close to the full lines which are now disclosed in the discovery of the more coherent 58b.

60 *Papyri Oxyrhynchus* 1787.
Fragmentary text is from the right column, lines 1–9.

62 *Papyri Oxyrhynchus* 1787 frag. 3 col. 2.3–14.

63 *Papyri Oxyrhynchus* 1787 frag. 3 col. 2.15–24.

65 *Papyri Oxyrhynchus* 1787 frag. 4. Treu p. 62.
Aheron (Acheron), the river of death, runs through Hades.

67a *Papyri Oxyrhynchus* 1787 frag. 5.
For Sappho and Homer, the Greek word for *daimon* (*daemon*)
meant a god. In later Greek, *daimon* meant a daemon or demon.
Only these four lines of the fragment are intelligible.

68a *Papyri Oxyrhynchus* 1787 frag. 7 + frag. nov. (Lobel S. M.,
p. 32 + *Papyri Oxyrhynchus* 21.135).
The poem is obscurely fragmentary. The sons of Tyndareus
are Kastor and Polydeukis. See "Tyndareus" in the glossary.
Megara is a friend of Sappho.

70 *Papyri Oxyrhynchus* 1787 frag. 13. Voigt.
Here *hóron* means "dance" and also "chorus" or "choir" (from
horós). The Greek chorus in a play danced as they chanted. The
word *horós* persists in modern Greek (and also in Romanian and
Turkish, for "round dance"). Greek Jews took their *horós* to Israel,
where it became the national dance, called the *hora* or *horah*.
    "Harmony" may be the notion of harmony or Harmona, god-
dess of harmony and concord, closely associated with Afroditi.

71 Treu p. 64, *Papyri Oxyrhynchus* 1787 frag. 6 + frag. 21 Addenda,
p. 135.
Mika (or Mnasis) may be a shortened form for Sappho's friend
Mnasidika. The house of Penthilos may refer to a rival school
(*thiasos*) or, more likely, a rival political party and enemy of Sap-
pho's family. Pittakos, the tyrant of Lesbos, married into the house

of Penthilos, wedding the sister of a former leader, Drakon, son of Penthilos. It cannot be known what Sappho's intended word was in line 7. Ernst Diehl and Max Treu venture the reading of ἄη[δοι for nightingale, and Campbell reads ἄη[ται, "breezes."

73a *Papyri Oxyrhynchus* 1787 frag. 11.
In so few words left of a longer poem, the most certain and constant message one gathers from these clean and striking remnants is that of the nearness, constancy, and elusiveness of eros—love and desire.

74 *Papyri Oxyrhynchus* 1787 frag. novum; Voigt 74a (lines 2, 4), 74b (line 2), 74c (line 2).
From three columns of a fragment. The fragment makes sense in the way that haphazard words in a poetry word game may work together, but in this instance the fragments fit as a poignantly Sapphic description of the shepherd.

76 *Papyri Oxyrhynchus* 1787 frag. 12.

78 *Papyri Oxyrhynchus* 1787 frag. 10.
A short column of words, with no certainty of person or connections. Among many such incoherent splashes of words, this one is representative and delightful.

81 Athinaios *Scholars at Dinner* 15.674e (3.491 Kaibel) (see 4–7) + *Papyri Oxyrhynchus* 1787 frag. 33 (see 1–5).
"Sappho gives a more simple reason for wearing garlands [her lines follow] in which she urges all who offer sacrifice to wreathe their heads, since being adorned with flowers makes them more pleasing to the gods."

82a Hefaistion *Handbook of Meters* 11.5 (p. 36 Consbruch).

84 *Papyri Oxyrhynchus* 1787 frags. 37, 41. Voigt.
Fragment 84 also resembles Ezra Pound's imitation of Sappho,

which brought the Greek poet into his approved modernity. See fragment 4.

85 *Papyri Oxyrhynchus* 1787 frag. 35 and 38. 85A + 85B in Voigt.
A lot of scraps.

86 *Papyri Oxyrhynchus* 1787 frag. postmodo repertum=2166(d)1.
This fragment is probably a prayer to Afroditi, though Zeus of the Aegis (a goatskin shield or breast plate) is also mentioned in line two.

87e, f Voigt = 87 LP (16), (17); *Papyri Oxyrhynchus* 2166.

88b, a *Papyri Oxyrhynchus* 2290.
I've translated just words and phrases that have sense. Somehow, even the slightest words and phrases of Sappho yield her voice.

91 Hefaistion *Handbook of Meters* 11.5.
Irana may be understood as "peace," or as a person's name, the English version of which would be "Irena" or "Irene."

92 *Papyri Berlin* 9722 fol. 1; *Berliner Klassikertexte* 5.2, p. 12 + Diehl *Anthologia Lyrica Graeca* 1.4, p. 57s.
Only line beginnings are preserved.

94 *Papyri Berlin* 9722 fol. 2; *Berliner Klassikertexte* 5.2, p. 12ss + Lobel, p. 70.
One of Sappho's longer and more important personal statements, here she invents her way of bringing herself, through a dialogue with a friend, into a poem, evoking exquisite love and sexual memories of an idealized youth. Again, the parallel with Cavafy is striking: recollection of youth, now gone. Of course, Constantine Cavafy knew Sappho's poems, as he did all ancient Greek poetry, but his re-creation of antiquity was usually of late Hellenism, with certain obvious exceptions, such as his most famous poem, "Ithaki,"

which retells, as a metaphor of instruction, Homer's tale of Odysseus the adventurer and his return to his island, which, though poor, gave him the reason for his long adventures and his return. In all their parallel sensual poems, whether of immediacy or recollection, Sappho and Cavafy are utterly candid. But Sappho makes no excuses and reveals no self-consciousness of illicit or immoral behavior for her love of women, in contrast to Cavafy, who was daringly candid, always with an awareness that his poems carried a dangerous message, which in his lifetime was sorrowfully epitomized by the nature of his publications, all private pamphlets and small collections for friends, not for a general public, which would in his lifetime (1863–1933) have been an unforgivable scandal. Though Sappho herself a century after her death became a stock figure of Greek and later Roman comedy and satire because of her lesbianism, her homoerotic preference did not inhibit or color her own writing. And despite her detractors, she was still the favorite of Plato—that may be more tale than history—and certainly of all important Greek poets and all historians. She was universally seen as the greatest lyric poet of Greek and Roman antiquity.

95 *Papyri Berlin* 9722 fol. 2; *Berliner Klassikertexte* 5.2, p. 14s.

Sappho is probably responding to Gongyla, whose name appears as the only word in line 1 of the extant papyrus. It is uncertain whom (or what) the sign may refer to in line 2 of the translation. The remaining lines of the fragment hang together. Letters are missing from his name, but Hermis is probably invoked here. His name appears in full in fragment 141. Hermis guides the dead to the underworld.

96 (lines 1–20) *Papyri Berlin* 9722 fol. 5; *Berliner Klassikertexte* 5.2, p. 15ss+Lobel, p. 80.

It is presumed that this poem is addressed to Atthis. It has the outstanding qualities of fragment 94. It is not known who the "us" and "you" and "she" are. One can speculate that the "you" is Atthis, and that the "she" is Anaktoria, because Anaktoria was away in Sardis. Yet the names may be reversed or none of the names may be her intention, which can only be known if more of the text is discovered. In this mingling of Sappho and her friends, Sappho is the one who craves one who is far and one who is shining, and there is an impossible triangle of love, typically Sapphic.

A fascinating analysis of fragment 96 appears in Denys Page's *Sappho and Alcaeus,* in which the ungenerous master Greek scholar attacks Sappho's word and person. Page's introductory study of "the contents and character of Sappho's poetry" is a modern if not wholly felicitous milestone after centuries of awesome praise and foolish tactics for disguising the poet's overt love for other women. With flowing élan, authority, and cynicism he examines twelve poems. Page essentially rejects all earlier attempts to find important symbolic meaning in the poet's words. He contends that it is a "straightforward, simple poem without profundity or memorable language" (Page, p. 95). Fragment 96 has fared better with later commentators, who see passionate and luminously subtle lines in one of our major surviving ancient lyrics.

96 (lines 21–37 in Campbell 96).

See previous note on 96 for source. This fragment may be a separate poem or a later part of 96. It is placed here as a companion poem to others on Sappho's gods and goddesses. While the fragment does not continue the great sweep of the love triangle in 96, it is a powerful statement on its own, bringing in Adonis and Afroditi in words made evocatively mysterious by the chance remnants of a mutilated papyrus. Though very fragmentary, it is too beautiful to be discarded as another unintelligible cache of Sappho's words.

98a *Papyri Haun.* 301.

In this intimate domestic poem addressed to her daughter, Kleis, Sappho contrasts an artificial adornment with the natural, inexpensive ornament of a wreath of fresh flowers, which is more appropriate for one with light hair. It was necessary for a respectable woman to wear some kind of headgear.

98b *Papyri Mediol.* ed. Vogliano, Philol. 93 (1939) 277ss.

Another reference to Kleis's blond hair here in fragment 98b, a poem of exile, when an elaborate headband was probably more than Sappho could afford. Sappho and her family were apparently in exile around 600 B.C.E. The poem recalls the days when the Mytilinian ruler Myrsilos (who probably caused the exile of Sappho's family) may have been the tyrant of Lesbos. Headbands seem to be reminders of an island past not available because of banishment. The Kleanaktidai were of a family of rulers of Mytilini during Sappho's lifetime.

100 Pollux *Vocabulary* 7.73 (2.73 Bethe).

"In Book 5 of Sappho's lyric poem we find [line follows], which means that the material was of close-woven linen."

101 Athinaios *Scholars at Dinner* 9.410e (2.395 Kaibel).

"When Sappho in *Book 5* of her Lyric poems says to Afroditi, [poem follows], she means the handkerchief as an adornment for the head, as indicated also by Hekataios, or some other writer, in the book entitled *Guide to Asia* where he writes: 'Women wear handkerchiefs on their heads.'"

The reading is difficult. J. M. Edmonds gratuitously inserts Timas as the giftgiver mentioned in the third line. Ulrich von Wilamowitz-Moellendorff and Diehl find *Mnasis* in the poem. Page finds no specific friend mentioned at all. More recently, David A. Campbell also finds *Mnasis* in the jumble of letters that comprise the first word of line three. Though using "she" for the unknown friend would be safer, with uncertainty I follow in favor of *Mnasis*. One intertextual reason, perhaps a folly, on the side of Mnasis is that fragment 82a brings in Mnasidika, who may be the same Mnasis sending gifts in 101.

101a Voigt (Sappho) or 347a, line 3, and 347b LP (Alkaios) Dimitrios *On Style* 142 (p. 33 Radermacher).

"There are many examples of literary grace. Such grace may be due to the choice of words or metaphor, as in the lines about the cicada."

Lobel and Page assign the poem to Alkaios, while Voigt, in her reliable, recent edition of Sappho, assigns the fragment to Sappho. Older scholars attributed the fragment to Sappho, including the very early Heinrich Ludolf Ahrens and U. von Wilamowitz-Moellendorff, but as Denys Page points out in *Sappho and Alcaeus* (p. 303), these lines also appear in a longer, more resolved poem by Alkaios, which is itself an imitation of a passage in Hesiod's *Works and Days*. Page reasons that it is too much to suppose that both poets imitated Hesiod. Yet how do we know what these friends did? While the first two lines seem like typical Alkaian drinking songs, the next three are deeply Sapphic. And so, again, whoever is right about attribution, one camp or another, I think these haunting lines deserve their place among the fragments. Here is the longer poem 347a by Alkaios:

Summer Star

Wash your gullet with wine for the dogstar returns
with the heat of summer searing a thirsting earth.
The cicadas cry softly under high leaves, and pour down
shrill song incessantly from under their wings
the artichoke is in flower. Women are poisonous, men
feeble, since the dogstar parches their heads and
  knees . . .*

102 Hefaistion *Handbook of Meters* 10.5.

"The antispastic tetrameter catalectic is also common, in which only the second unit is antispastic, a meter in which Sappho wrote her songs at the end of *Book 7*: [verse follows]."

The speaker in the poem seems to be stricken by desire for a

* Willis Barnstone, trans., *Sappho and the Greek Lyric Poets* (New York: Schocken Books, 1987, p. 56). The dogstar is not the morning star but the dogstar Syrius that brings the heat and madness of the dog days.

young man. Afroditi, who caused the desire, is also brought in for her slender beauty.

103 *Papyri Oxyrhynchus* 2294.

This fragment consists of a list of first lines of poems by Sappho. In the Greek, therefore, they do not constitute one continuous poem.

103b *Papyri Oxyrhynchus* 2308 Voigt; incert. 26 LP.

103C a, b Voigt (lines 2, 4, 5, 7, 10, 12) with 214 Campbell (frag. 4, line 3). *Papyri Oxyrhynchus* 2357.

104a Dimitrios *On Style 141* (p. 33 Radermacher).

"Sappho also creates charm from the use of anaphora, as in this on the Evening Star: [her lines follow]. Here the charm lies in the repetition of the word 'bring.' "

The Evening Star, son of Astraios or Kephalos or Atlas and Eos (Dawn), and father of the Hesperides.

Many poets have imitated this fragment, from Catullus's poem 62 (lines 20–37) to Byron in *Don Juan*, canto 3, stanza 107:

> O Hesperus, thou bringest all good things—
> Home to the weary, to the hungry cheer,
> To the young bird the parent's brooding wings,
> The welcome stall to the o'erlaboured steer;
> Whate'er of peace about our hearthstone clings,
> Whate'er our household gods protect of dear,
> Are gathered round us by thy look of rest;
> Thou bring'st the child too to its mother's breast.

104b Himerios *Declamations* 46.8 (p. 188 Colonna).

"This song to Hesperos is by Sappho."

105a, c Syrianos on Hermogenis' *On Kinds of Style* 1.1 (Rabe).

"Some kinds of style have to do with one kind of thought only. . . . Others . . . express things pleasing to the senses of sight, hearing, smell, taste, touch, such as Sappho's [verse follows]."

Himerios *Declamations* 9–16.

"Sappho compared a virgin girl to an apple, not allowing those who would pluck it before its time even to touch it with their fingertips, but he who would pick it in the right season might watch its beauty grow; she compared the bridegroom to Achilles and his deeds to the hero's."

Dimitrios *On Style* 106 (p. 26 Radermacher).

"The epiphonema, as it is called, may be considered as a phrase that adds adornment, and elevates style. . . . For example, the sense is intensified by such a phrase as "like a hyacinth" . . . , while it is adorned by the succeeding words "and on the earth the purple flower." "

Sappho's words are echoed in Catullus 11.21–24, and Virgil *Aeneid* 9.435.

106 Dimitrios *On Style* 146.
"Of this outstanding man Sappho says: [verse follows]."

107 Apollonios Dyskolos *On Conjunctions* 490 (1.223 Schneider).
"In all dialects except Koine and Attic, ἄρα has the form ἦρα as in Sappho: [verse follows]."

108 Himerios *Orations* 9.19 (p. 84 Colonna). Voigt.
Himerios the rhetorician writes, "Then come and we will lead him into the bedroom and urge him to gaze on the beauty of the virgin bride. [Verse follows.] The praises of the Lesbian woman befit you."

110 Hefaistion *Handbook of Meters* 7.6. (p. 23 Consbruch).
"The Aiolic dactylic tetrameter catalectic: [verse follows]."

Synesios *Letters* 3.158d.
"The man who is wronged is Harmonios, the father of the head doorkeeper, who, as Sappho would say (though in other

respects he lived soberly and honestly), claimed to be better born than Kekrops himself."

Dimitrios *On Style* 167 (p. 37 Radermacher).

"In a different way Sappho ridicules the rustic groom and the doorkeeper at the wedding, using prosaic rather than poetic language."

Elsewhere the second-century scholar Pollux says that the doorkeeper kept the bride's friends from rescuing her.

111 Hefaistion *On Poems* 7.1 (p. 70 Consbruch); Dimitrios *On Style* 148 (p. 34 Radermacher). Voigt.

"When the refrain occurs not after a stanza but after a line and is followed by another line, it is called a 'mesymnion,' a 'central refrain,' as for example in Sappho: [verse follows]."

There is a charm peculiarly Sapphic in its way when having said something, she changes her mind, as if interrupting herself because she has resorted to an impossible hyperbole, for no one really is as tall as Aris. Some scholars and translators add a last line, which repeats the refrain "Hymenaios!." J. D. Salinger's brief novel, *Raise High the Roof Beam, Carpenters and Seymour: An Introduction*, took its title from the first line of Sappho's lyric poem 111.

112 Hefaistion *Handbook of Meters* 15.26 (p. 55s Consbruch).

"The same poet uses the 3 1/2-foot choriambic with an iambic close: [verse follows]."

113 Dionysios of Halikarnassos *On Literary Composition* 25 (6.127s Usener-Radermacher).

"A Sapphic wedding song."

114 Dimitrios *On Style* 140 (p. 33 Radermacher).

"The graces that arise from the use of figures of speech are many and clear in Sappho as for example, when a bride addresses virginity and, using the same figure, her virginity replies. [Verse follows.]"

115 Hefaistion *Handbook of Meters* 7.6. (p. 23 Consbruch).
"And the Aiolic dactylic pentameters, catalectic with a disyllabic ending."

118 Hermogenis *On Kinds of Oratory*; 2.4 (p. 334 Rabe).
"The assignment of something deliberately chosen with respect to things that do not have the power of deliberate choice produces a sweet effect . . . as when Sappho questions her lyre and the lyre answers her: [verse follows]."

120 *Etymologicum Magnum* 2.43.
"Βάζω, 'I say,' . . . from it comes ἀβακής, 'unspeaking,' 'quiet,' 'gentle,' which Sappho uses in [verse follows]."
Catullus has phrases reminiscent of these lines: *mellitos oculos* (48.1) and *Pulcher es, neque to Venus neglegit* (61.194).

121 Stobaios *Anthology* 4.22.112 (6.543 Wachsmuth-Hense).
"In marriage it is best that the ages of the partners should be considered. Sappho [verse follows]."

122 Athinaios *Scholars at Dinner* 12.554b (3.223 Kaibel).
"It is natural that those who see beauty and ripeness in themselves should gather flowers. That is why Persefoni and her companions are described as gathering flowers. Sappho says she saw: [verse follows]."

123 Ammonios *On Similar Words That Also Differ* 75 (p. 19 Nickau).
"There is a difference between ἀρτι and αρτίως. ἀρτι is an adverb of time, while αρτίως is applied to a completed action. So Sappho was wrong when she said: [verse follows]."

125 Scholiast on Aristophanes' *Thesmoforiazusai* 401 (p. 267 Dübner).
"The young and people in love wove garlands. Here is a reference to the custom of those women who in old days wore garlands. As in Sappho: [verse follows]."

126 *Etymologicum Gen. (papyri Calame)* = *Etymologicum Magnum* 250.10s.

"*daúo tò koimômai*, 'sleep,' in Sappho."

Herodian says that this word [for sleep] occurs only once in Sappho.

127 Hefaistion *Handbook of Meters* 15.25 (p. 55 Consbruch).

"Sappho composed the line containing two ithyphallics: [verse follows]."

The "gold house" may be the house of Zeus.

128 Hefaistion *Handbook of Meters* 9.2. (p. 30 Consbruch).

"The choriambic tetrameter, found in longer sequences, as in Sappho's lines that begin: [verse follows]."

129a, b Apollonios Dyskolos *Pronouns* 66.3 (1.66 Schneider).

"ἔμεθεν ["of me"] is often used by the Aiolic poets: [verse follows]."

130 Hefaistion *Handbook of Meters* 7.7 (p. 23 Consbruch).

"The Aiolic dactylic tetrameter acatalectic is as follows: [verse follows]."

Maximus of Tyre, *Orations*, 18.9 (p. 232 Hobein).

"Diotima says [in Plato's *Symposium*] that Eros flowers in prosperity and dies in want. Sappho put these together and called him 'sweetbitter.'"

These two lines may be followed by fragment 131.

131 Hefaistion *Handbook of Meters* 7.7 (see ad frag. 130); Plutarch, *Dialogue on Love*, 751d.

132 Hefaistion *Handbook of Meters* 1.5.18 (p. 53s Consbruch).

The fragment is preceded and followed by prosodic matters, especially concerning meter (four kinds of trochaic dimeters) and the use of caesura.

It cannot be known what noun should follow "lovely," but Campbell and others have guessed "Lesbos."

133a, b Hefaistion *Handbook of Meters* 14.7 (p. 46 Consbruch).

"When the ionic is anaclastic [meaning it has its syllables inverted], it is preceded by an iambic of six or seven short units, giving us: [two lines follow]."

Lines a and b are probably from the same poem, and line a may have been the first line of that poem. It is not known what verb connected the questioning "why" and Afroditi. Others have guessed "condemn" or "honor" or "neglect" or "summon," but we have no reasonable basis for this conjecture other than that a word is missing, indicating an intended relationship between Sappho and Afroditi.

134 Hefaistion *Handbook of Meters* 12.4 (p. 39 Consbruch).

"Among ionic *a* minore acatalectic trimeters is the acatlectic in Sappho's: [verse follows]."

The one "born in Kypros" is Afroditi.

135 Hefaistion *Handbook of Meters* 12.2 (p. 37s Consbruch).

"Whole songs are written in ionics, as for example those by Alkman and Sappho: [line follows]."

Irana (in English, Irene), as well as being a personal name, means "peace."

136 Scholiast on Sophocles *El.* 149 (p. 110 Papageorg).

"The phrase 'messenger' or 'herald of Zeus' is used because the nightingale signals the coming of spring. Sappho writes: [line follows]."

Ben Jonson took from this fragment his line in *The Sad Shepherd*, act 2: "The dear good angel of the Spring, the Nightingale." He gave Sappho's word *angelos*, herald, or messenger, its later biblical meaning of "angel."

137 Aristotle *Rhetoric* 1367e (p. 47s Römer).

"We are ashamed of what is shameful, whether it is said, done or intended; compare Sappho's answer when Alkaios said: 'I want to speak to you but shame disarms me.'"

The poem is addressed to the fellow Lesbian poet Alkaios (Alcaeus in Latin), to whom is attributed the line: "Violet-haired, holy, honeysmiling Sappho." Sappho's lines are said to be her response. All this is uncertain, though there is little doubt that the rebuke of the poet is indeed by Sappho.

138 Athinaios *Scholars at Dinner* 13.56d (3.244 Kaibel).

"And Sappho also says to the man who is excessively admired for his beauty: [verse follows]."

139 Philo *Papyri Oxyrhynchus* 1356 fol. 4a 14ss + Lobel, p. 55.

"Yielding to the good counsel of the woman poet Sappho concerning the gods."

140 Hefaistion *Handbook of Meters* 10.4 (p. 33 Consbruch).

"Among antispastic tetrameters the following is the pure form of catalectic line."

Kythereia is Afroditi. The verses are probably a dialogue between Afroditi and her worshipers. The lines addressed to Afroditi are probably by worshipers of an Adonis cult. See 168.

141a, b Athinaios *Scholars at Dinner* 10.425d (3.425 Kaibel).

"According to some versions, the wine-bearer of the gods was Harmonia. Alkaios makes Hermis also the wine-bearer, as does Sappho, who says: [verse follows]."

142 Athinaios *Scholars at Dinner* 13.571d (3.259s Kaibel).

"Free women and young girls even today call their intimate and loving friends ἑταίρας (*hetaira* or *hetaera*, meaning "companions") as Sappho does: [verse follows]."

In later Greek, *hetaira* meant an educated "courtesan" or "mistress."

143 Athinaios *Scholars at Dinner* 2.54f (1.127s Kaibel).

144 Herodianos *On the Declension of Nouns* (ap. Aldi *Thes. Cornu-copia* 268; see Choerob. 2.65 43s Hilgard)=cod. Voss. g. 20 (Reit-zenstein *Gesch. E.* 367).
Gorgo is a rival of Sappho's.

146 Tryfon *Figures of Speech* 25 (*Rhet. Gr.* 8.760 Walz), *Diogenianos Proverbs* 6.58 (1.279 Leutsch-Schneidewin).
"[Sappho] said of those who are unwilling to take the bitter with the sweet."
The fragment is normally said to reflect the proverb of Diogenianos concerning those not willing to accept the bad with the good, but here she seems to say she chooses neither honey nor the bee.

147 Dio Chrysoston *Discourses* 37.47 (2.29 Arnim).
"'Someone, I tell you, will remember us,' as Sappho has beautifully said. . . . The lines in brackets derive from Dio Chrysostom's summary of Sappho's words. Up to now forgetfulness has tripped and cheated others, but good judgment has not cheated anyone of worth."

148 Scholiast on Pindar's *Olympian Odes* 2.96f (1.85s Drachmann).
"The meaning: Wealth when not by itself but embellished by virtue, opportunely enjoys its own benefits and that of virtue [*arete*], and has a wise concern for the pursuit of the good. Neither of these on its own is welcome."
The text is uncertain, and the second line might not be Sappho's.

149 Apollonios Dyskolos *Pronouns* 126b (1.99 Schneider); 151: *Etymologicum Genuinum* (p. 19 Calame) = *Etymologicum Magnum* 117.14ss.
"And σφι ['to them'] is used in Aiolic with an initial ἄ: [line follows]."

150 Maximus of Tyre *Orations* 24.18.9 (p. 232 Hobein).
"Socrates blazed up in anger with Xanthippe for lamenting when he was near death as Sappho did with her daughter: [poem follows]."

151 See 149.
"ἄωρος is a lengthened form of ὧρος, which has the same meaning, 'sleep.' See Kallimahos (fr. 177.28 Pf.) and Sappho." See fragment 149.

152 Scholiast on Apollonios of Rhodes 1.727 (p. 61 Wendel).
"ἐρευθήσσα, 'red,' is used instead of πυσσα, 'flame-colored,' or ὑπέρυθσος, 'ruddy.' This is contradictory to Sappho's description: [verse follows]."

153 Atilius Fortunatianus. Ars 28 (vi 301 Keil) (*de metris Horatii*).
In his comment on a poem by Horace, "Ode 1.8," beginning *Lydia dic per omnes*, Atilius Fortunatianus cites this phrase by Sappho.

154 Hefaistion *Handbook of Meters* 11.3 (p. 35 Consbruch) (on the ionic a major).
"And there are brachycatalectic trimeters that are called praxilleans. They have an ionic in the first meter and a trochaic in the second. Compare this example from Sappho: [verse follows]."

155 Maximus of Tyre *Orations* 18.9d (p. 231 Hobein).
"Sometimes she censures them (Gorgo and Andromeda), sometimes she questions them, and just like Socrates she uses irony. Socrates says, [in the opening line of Plato's *Ion*,] "Good day to you, Ion," and Sappho says: [verse follows]."

156 Dimitrios *On Style* 161s (p. 37 Radermacher).
"The charm of comedy lies especially in hyperbole, and each hyperbole is an impossibility . . . such as Sappho's [verse follows]."

Dimitrios *On Style* 127 (p. 30 Radermacher).

"Sappho's praise as in 'More gold than gold' is certainly a hyperbole and contains an impossibility, but is not without elegance. Moreover, it derives its charm from the impossible. Indeed, the wondrous in holy Sappho is that she uses a device that is hazardous and difficult."

Grigorios of Korinthos on Hermogenis *Meth. (Rhet. Gr.* 7.1236 Walz).

"The ear is lowly flattered by phrases such as those by Anakreon and Sappho, as in 'whiter than milk,' 'gentler than water,' 'more melodious than lyres,' 'prouder than a mare,' 'more delicate than roses,' 'more precious than gold.'"

Unfortunately, we do not know which of these comparisons are by Anakreon and which by Sappho, yet the statement here in Grigorios is somehow valuable as a lost glint of possibility.

157 *Etymologicum Genuinum*

"ανôς, ἠώς, this is the Aiolic form. See Sappho: [phrase follows] and fragment 104a."

158 Plutarch *On Restraining Anger* 7.456e (3.167 Pohlenz-Sieveking).

"A man who is silent over his wine is boring and vulgar, and in anger there is nothing more dignified than tranquility, as Sappho advises."

158 Diehl *Greek Anthology* 7.489.

Diehl includes three poems from the Hellenistic period, clearly in imitation of Sappho, though the prosody is of the epigrammatic style of the *Greek Anthology*, also called the *Palantine Anthology*. The first of the poems from the *Greek Anthology*, beginning "Children, I am voiceless," is not remotely Sappho's in style and offers nothing about Sappho. Its only connections are the false ascription to Sappho and the mention of Aithopia, who is Artemis in a Lesbian cult.

159 Maximus of Tyre, *Orations*, 18.9g (p. 232 Hobein)
"Diotima [in Plato's *Symposium*] tells Socrates that Eros is not the son but the attendant and servant of Afroditi, and in a poem Afroditi sings to Sappho."

159 Diehl *Greek Anthology* 7.505.

160 Athinaios *Scholars at Dinner* 13.571d (see frag. 142).
See comments on *hetaira* in note 142.

161 *Papyri Bouriant* 8.91ss (column 62ss).

166 Athinaios *Scholars at Dinner* 2.57 (1.134 Kaibel).
"Sappho makes ὤόν, 'egg,' trisyllabic [ὤόιν]: [verse follows]."

167 Athinaios *Scholars at Dinner* 2.57d.
See note on fragment 166.

168 Marius Plotius Sacerdos *Art of Grammar* 3.3 (see vi 516 Keil).
"Sappho invented the adonius or catalectic dimeter, so it is also known as Sapphic. It is monoschematic, since it is always composed of a dactyl and a spondee." See 140.

168b Campbell (frag. adesp. 976 P.M.G.); Hefaistion *Handbook of Meters* 11.5 (on ionic tetrameters acatalectic) (p. 37 Consbruch).
Although this is one of the two or three best-known poems attributed to Sappho, there is a lot of fuss about whether it is by Sappho, by Alkaios, or by neither, and most recent editors deny her authorship, though it is included in most Greek editions under the epithet of "incert." Apart from authorship, the poem is a simple yet impeccable example of images of loneliness.
Earlier scholars, including Arsenius around 1500, said yes, this is Sappho, and then later ones, from Wilamowitz to Lobel and

Page, said no. My own thought is that it is quintessential Sappho, whatever the uncertainty of scholarship. I remember a fuming, hilarious letter to me from the formidable pioneer translator of Greek poetry and drama, Dudley Fitts, who was having a fit over this essential poem. So feelings arise.

I preferred in the translation to follow the Greek word order, placing the Pleiades in the second line, leaving it ambiguous, meaning it may signify that the moon and Pleiades have set, or more likely that the moon has set and suddenly also the Pleiades.

168c (frag. adesp. 964 P.M.G.); Dimitrios *On Style* (p. 37 Radermacher).

"Grace is produced in keeping with ornamentation and by using beautiful words that contribute to it as in: [lines follow]."

The scholar Ulrich von Wilamowitz and Lobel and Page attribute the lines to Sappho. Other modern scholars dissent, but whether Sappho or not, these exquisite lines fit the Sapphic fragments.

178 Zenobios *Proverbs* 3.3 (1.58 Leutsch-Schneidewin).

Zenobios cites the poem and then says:

"This is a saying used about those who died prematurely, or of those who like children but ruin them by how they bring them up. Gello was a girl. She died prematurely, and Lesbians say that her ghost haunts little children, and they blame premature deaths on her. Sappho mentions her."

201 Aristotle *Rhetoric* 1398b.

The words are Aristotle's restatement, how close we cannot know, of Sappho's words. Aristotle's words are not originally lineated as two verses in the Greek, but are done so here to match the English.

204 Scholiast on Pindar, *Pythian Odes* 4.410c (2.153 Drachmann).

"Gold is indestructible, Sappho says . . . and Pindar says that gold is the child of Zeus."

The second-century geographer and traveler also notes, in *Description of Greece* 8.18 (2 301 Spiro), "That gold is not corrupted by the rust is confirmed by the Lesbian poet [Sappho] and also proved by the metal itself."

METRICAL GUIDE

by William E. McCulloh, Kenyon College

A POEM IN GREEK emerges from a fundamental pulsation; its words
live in rhythmic phrases. In Sappho's lyric poetry, the rhythms
were embedded in music and were sung by the poet. The verse
patterns available to the Greek lyric poet were abundant beyond
anything known in English poetry. The metrical guide provided
below aims to help those who can pronounce Greek but have no
experience with the lyric meters. Those who seek an introduction
to the subject should start with *The Meters of Greek and Latin Po-
etry* by James W. Halporn, Martin Ostwald, and Thomas G.
Rosenmeyer. For the best current full presentation, they should
proceed to *Greek Metre* by M. L. West.

Ancient Greek verse was structured by the relative lengths of
the syllables in a line, not by the arrangement of stressed and
unstressed syllables. Syllables were either long or short. A long
syllable was equal to two short ones. With a few exceptions,
syllables containing the vowels η and ω and diphthongs were
always long. α, ι, and υ were sometimes long, sometimes short,
depending on the particular word. ε and o were short. But when
any short vowel was immediately followed by two consonants
(either in the same word or at the beginning of the next), the
combination almost invariably—for Sappho—produced a long
syllable.

Note these irregularities: (1) A short syllable at the end of a
line was allowed to stand in place of a long syllable. (2) If one
vowel was immediately followed in the next syllable by another
vowel, the two could on occasion be slurred together—even
from the end of one word to the beginning of the next. (3) In

some dactylic meters, a long vowel or diphthong at the end of a word could be shortened if the following word began with a vowel. (4) At certain points in some verse forms, usually at or near the beginning, either long or short syllables could be used.

The poems of Sappho were probably divided into nine books, of which the first four and perhaps two others each had its own particular verse form. The tables below follow this division, with a tenth group for poems of uncertain location. The classification by books (including the group of uncertain location) follows that of the Lobel-Page edition and of Denys Page's "Appendix on Metres" in *Sappho and Alcaeus* (see Bibliography).

Many of the fragments exhibit only a portion of their original meter, but to one who knows that meter, even a scrap can come to life. Consider what the following English fragments gain if one knows of their full metrical form:

> . . . . all through the house
> . . . . . creature was stirring, not even a . . .
>
> . . . . walk a little faster, said the whiting to the . . .
> . . . . and it's treading on my tail.
>
> . . . . sat on a wall,
> . . . . . . Dumpty had a great . . . . .

When the meter of a fragment is as yet uncertain or unknown, I have nevertheless tried to indicate the rhythm of what we have, except in a few instances of extreme fragmentation or corruption. These instances are marked with an asterisk (*). Although Books I through IV each have a specific meter, some fragments therein are too small to bring into relation with that meter.

Signs

   _ long syllable

   u short syllable

x either long or short

| end of metrical phrase within a line (indicated mostly in the group of uncertain location)

/ division between lines

(Note: spacing has sometimes been used to suggest grouping of smaller metrical units within the line.)

It is best to become familiar with at least these frequently used metrical components, so that the verses may be read as the focused patterns they are, rather than just a shapeless succession of long and short syllables:

da = dactyl: _uu

sp = spondee: _ _

ch = choriamb: _uu_

cr = cretic: _u_

ba = bacchiac: u_ _

gl = glyconic: xx_uu_u_

Compare Algernon Swinburne's "Fly, white butterflies, out to sea," which follows this pattern. The following variant forms sometimes occur: "gl: _uu_u_u_ or gl": _u_u_uu_. In West's notation the position of " is used to indicate, as he says, "whether the double short comes earlier or later than its normal place." (See West 1982, 31.)

Book I

Poems in Sapphic stanza. This stanza is usually printed as four lines (but would more accurately be represented as three, since line 4 is continuous with line 3).

_u_x_uu_u_ _

_u_x_uu_u_ _

_u_x_uu_u_ _

_uu_ _

Poems 1–42 belong to this book. (Ten, which are exceedingly fragmentary or brief, have been omitted here: 8, 10–14, 25, 28–29, 35.)

Book II

Each line consists of a glyconic with two inserted dactyls: gl²ᵈᵃ

xx_uu _uu _uu_u_

Poems 43–52 belong here.

Book III

The lines are grouped in pairs. (This is not indicated in current editions of Sappho.) Each line consists of a glyconic with two inserted choriambs: gl²ᶜʰ

xx_uu_ _uu_ _uu_u_

Poems 53–57 belong here.

Book IV

Paired lines. (In some fragments the pairing is not now ascertainable.) Each line has either a long or short syllable (x) followed by three choriambs and a bacchiac: x ch ch ch ba

x_uu_ _uu_ _uu_ u_ _

This meter resembles that of Book III, except for the missing syllable at the beginning and the extra syllable at the end.

Poems 58–91 belong here, except number 88 (see Lobel-Page 1955, 86n). The following have been omitted as excessively fragmentary: 59, 61, 64, 66, 69, 72, 75, 77, 79–80, 83, 90. (There is no text at all for 89.)

Book V

Poems composed in various three-line stanzas based on the glyconic (except for 101a):

Poems 92–101 (omitted: 93, 97, 99).

92*

94 gl / gl / gl^(da) (glyconic with inserted dactyl)

95 cr gl / gl /gl ba (line 3: "gl; line 6: gl")

96 (lines 1–20) like 95 (line 7 gl")

96 (lines 21–37) like 95

98a gl / gl / cr gl

98b like 98a

100 _u_ _ _ ... [_?]uu_ ch_

101 gl? / gl / ? / gl?

101a xx_uu_ _uu_ _uu_u_ (gl²ᶜʰ) If this fragment is by Sappho (which is debatable), this would belong metrically in Book III.

Book VI

As Page says, there is no evidence for Book VI. (See Page 1959, 320.)

Book VII

102 u_u_u_ _ | uu_u_u_ _

Book VIII

103 lines 2–8, 10: ch ch ch ba ? (The meter of line 1 is not identifiable; line 9 would require emendation; see Page 1959, 118.)

103b*

103Ca, b*

Book IX

Epithalamia (Wedding Songs) in various meters:

Poems 104–117 (omitted: 109, 116, 117)

104a dactylic hexameter: da da da da da _ _

104b _u_ _ _u_ _ | u [= _?]

105a, c dactylic hexameter (see 104a). In this meter a spondee often takes the place of a dactyl:

sp da da da da _ _ (lines a 1; c 1)
sp da sp da da _ _ (line a 3)

106 dactylic hexameter (see 104a)

107 dactylic hexameter? (incomplete; Page 1959, 123)

108 dactylic hexameter? (incomplete; Page 1959, 123)

110 xx da da _ _

111 _ _ da _ _

u_u_ lines 2, 4, 6, 8
x da da _ _ lines 3, 7

112 ch ba | ch ba

113 if emended, possibly _ _ _uu_uu_ _uu_ _ (Page 1959, 124)

114 ch ch ch ba (like Book VIII?)

115 xx da da da _ _ (like Book II, except for missing penultimate)

Fragments of uncertain location

118 gl u_? / gl ?

120 ch ch u_
_ _ ch ch

121 xx_uu_ _ / gl / gl / gl

122 _uu_ _ _ | _u_uu_

123 _u_u_ | ch ba

125] _uu_u_

126 _ ch ba | _ _u u [

127 _u_u_ _ | _u_u_ _

128 ch ch ch ba (like Book VIII?)

129a, b uu_u_u_ _

  _u_u_ _ | _uu_u_ _

130 gl^{da}

131 gl^{da}

132 line 1: _u_u_u_ | _u_u_u_ _

  line 2: _u_u_u_ | _uu_u_ _

  line 3 = line 1 (if emended as Page suggests, 1959, 131—32n4)

133a, b x_u_ | uu_u_u_ _

134 uu_u_u_ _ | uu_ _ (West 1982, 31n4)

135 uu_ _ uu_ _ uu_ _

136 xx da da da _ _ (compare 115)

137 Alcaic stanza—the stanza form frequently used by Alkaios, Sappho's contemporary compatriot:

  x_u_x_uu_u_

  x_u_x_uu_u_

  x_u_x_u_ _

  _uu_uu_u_ _

Lines 1–2 are a fragment of a stanza. Line 5 is metrically corrupt.

138 Fragment of an Alcaic stanza (see 137)

139*

140 xx ch ch ch _

141a, b lines 1 and 4: _ _uu_ _

    lines 2 and 5: _ _u_ _

    line 3: _ _u_ _ | _u_u _uu_ _

    line 6: _ _u_ _ | _uu_ u_ _

142 dactylic hexameter: sp da da da da _ _

143 (See 142.)

144 uu_uu_u_

146 xx da da _ _

147 _ _ _uu_u [

148*

149 uu da da _ _

150 x ch ch [

    _u_u_ _ | _u_u_

151 xx ch ch _

152 _uu_uu_u_uu_ _

153 ch ba

154 x ch u_u_ _

155 _u_ _ | da da _u_ _

156 uu da da cr

    _ _ _uu_

157 _uu_ _

158 ch _ | ch _

159 [_?]uu_ ch u_

160 cr ch ba

161*

166 xx ch ch u_ (gl^ch)

   ch ch u_

167 xx da da _

168 _uu_ _

168b x ch ba

168c _ _u_ _

   da da _

178 gl

Fragments either by Sappho or by Alkaios ("incertum")

5a gl^2da ? (like Book II)

5b*

5c*

13 _u_ _ | _

16 x ch ch ba

18b, c] uu_u_u_ _

25 da da da da _ _ (incomplete dactylic hexameter?)

27] ch ba [(lines 1 and 2)

Elegiac Poems Wrongly Attributed to Sappho

These are composed in elegiac couplets.

D 159 sp da da da da _ _ (dactylic hexameter)
     sp sp _ | da da _ (so-called pentameter)

D 158 da da sp da da _ _ (dactylic hexameter)
     da da _ | da da _ (so-called pentameter)
     da da sp da da _ _
     da sp _ | da da _

GLOSSARY

When numbers appear at the end of an entry, they indicate poems in which the glossary term appears.

ABANTHIS. Nothing is known of Abanthis. 22.

ADONIS. A handsome young god of vegetation and fertility. Because of his beauty, both Afroditi and Persefoni (Persephone) coveted young Adonis as a lover. He was identified with the seeding and harvesting of crops and was worshiped especially by women. When Adonis was killed by the tusks of a wild boar, Afroditi and Persefoni each wanted him as her lover. Zeus intervened and assigned him to spend half the year with Afroditi aboveground in the summer months and the other half with Persefoni down in Hades. Other versions give Adonis four months with each of the courting women and four months alone or with his choice companion. Adonis's death and resurrection were celebrated in festivals in Greece as a symbol of the yearly cycle of vegetation. Some say that the boar that killed Adonis was sent by his lover, the chaste Artemis, or by her lover, Aris, who was jealous of Adonis's beauty. Each drop of Adonis's blood turned into a blood red flower, the anemone.

Adonis as a lord of fertility goes back to Mesopotamian roots, including his worship among the Phrygians as Attis and among the Babylonians as Tammuz. The word *adonis* means "lord," a Semitic word found in Aramaic and Hebrew that has entered many Indo-European languages. In the Hebrew Bible *adonai* means "my lord" and is, along with Yahweh (the tetragrammaton YHWH) and Ha Shem (the name), a name for nameless God. In Spanish, *don*, from *adonis*, is a male honorific title, as in Don Quijote, and *doña* is a feminine title, as in Doña Perfecta. In Italian, *adonis* has given us the honorifics *donna* and *donatello* (little lord). 140, 168.

AFRODITI (Aphrodite; Afrodita in Sappho's Aiolic speech). A goddess of love, beauty, sea, flowers, and fertility. In Homer, Afroditi is the daughter of Zeus and Dioni. She was born in the sea foam (*afros*) off the shore of Paphos in Kypros (Cyprus), but that froth consisted of blood and semen dropped into the sea after Kronos castrated Ouranos (Uranus), god of the sky. To keep her in check, Zeus compelled the goddess of desire to marry the ugly Hefaistos (Hephestus), the god of fire and the forge, who is Vulcan in Roman mythology. Afroditi was bored with the metalworker. When Hefaistos found her and Aris in a lovers' embrace, he locked them in an iron net. But from her union with Aris she bore Harmona and, in some versions, also Anteros and Eros. By Hermis she bore Hermafroditos, and by Dionysos she was the mother of phallic Priapos. The Romans inherited a deific past when Zeus caused her to fall in love with the shepherd Anchises, whose offspring was Aeneas, the later Roman hero. Her star affair was with the beautiful youth Adonis, whom Persefoni also desired. Zeus arranged for the jealous goddesses to share Adonis, giving six (or four) months' possession to each.

Afroditi had an important cult at Kythereia on Kriti (see poems 2, 86, and 140). She was often accompanied by her son Eros, also a god of love and desire. As a symbol of passion and romantic love, she is a particular ally to Sappho and is mentioned by Sappho in the existing fragments more often than any other deity or person. The complete poem attributed to Sappho (fragment 1) is addressed to Afroditi. Sappho calls her variously Kypris (Cypris), Kyprian (Cyprian), Kypros-born (Cyprus-born), the Pafian (Paphian) of Pafos (Paphos), and Kythereia.

Earlier, in Mesopotamia, she was Astarte and Ishtar, while in Rome she was Venus. 1; 2; 33; 44; 65; 73a; 87e, f; 95; 96; 101; 102; 112; 133a, b; 159; 168.

AHERON (Acheron). The river of death running through Hades. It began in Thesprotia, Epeiros, and disappeared underground in places where it was supposed to lead to Hades. *Aheron* is frequently a synonym of *Hades*. 95.

ALKAIOS (Alcaeus). Born about 620 B.C.E. in Mytilini (Lesbos), the poet was a contemporary and possible friend or lover of Sappho's. He wrote, in the Aiolic (Lesbian) dialect, lyric poems that deal with politics, love, drinking, the sea. The ship-of-state poem, made famous by Horace, is earliest found in the poems of Alkaios. The best-known modern version is Walt Whitman's "Oh Captain, My Captain," whose origin goes directly back to Lesbian Alkaios. Alkaios was of an aristocratic family in Lesbos, and when the enemy Pittakos became the tyrant (ruler), Alkaios and his family went into exile. 137.

ANAKTORIA. One of Sappho's friends. One theory is that she left Sappho in order to marry and follow her husband to Sardis, where he was probably a soldier. 16.

ANDROMACHE (Andromáhi). Her name is composed of *andros*, meaning "man," and *máhi*, meaning "battle" or "war." She was the wife of Hektor, the Trojan hero, who was killed by Achilles. Later the princess widow married Hektor's brother Helenos, and they ruled jointly in Epeiros (Epirus), present-day northwestern Greece and Albania. Homer is evenhanded in treating Achaians and Trojans, portraying Andromache as a noble figure. Sappho celebrates her, and she is the tragic heroine of plays by Euripides and Racine. 44.

ANDROMEDA. A rival of Sappho's; perhaps a poet. 68a; 131; 133a, b.

APOLLO. Apollo the sun god and his twin sister Artemis the moon god were born in Delos, the children of Zeus and Lito (Leto). He was a god of prophecy, music, medicine, archery. He was also the ideal of young, manly beauty, and connected with philosophy and all the arts. For mystery religions and gnosticism, he was Phoebus, the god of light.

Apollo's failed in his attempt to seduce Dafni (Daphne), known as Laura to the Romans. Dafni turned herself into a laurel tree (*dafni*, in Greek) rather than yield to him. He ran off like a lowly hound, as Ovid writes, but fooled himself into believing himself victorious by seizing leaves of the laurel tree and crowning himself with them as a sign of his conquest: hence, the Olympic laurel leaves today signify victory.

There were many shrines to worship the sun god, the major oracular and athletic one being at Delfi, where the Pythian Games were held in his honor every four years. Apollo is above all identified with perfection, beauty, and art. In this he was the leader of the Muses, directing their choir. His attributes included the lyre (cithara) and plectrum, as well as swans, wolves, dolphins, and bows and arrows. The "far-shooting archer" was one of his titles. He was also a god of prophecy and medicine. In literature his golden-mean qualities are often contrasted to those of his brother Dionysos. In *The Birth of Tragedy*, Nietzsche contrasts Dionysian madness and inspiration to Apollonian measure, harmony, and reason.

Sappho's poem on the wedding of Andromache and Hektor ends with a thrilling paean, which is a hymn sung to Apollo. Among Apollo's many epithets were Phoebus and Paean. Sappho called him Paon, the Aiolic form of Paean (Paian). 44.

ARIS (Ares). Aris, the fierce Olympian war god, was the son of Zeus and Hera, though in one legend he and his twin sister, Eris, were born when Hera touched a flower. He fought gods and mortals. When Poseidon's son violated Aris' daughter, Aris killed him. For his crime he was brought to trial and acquitted before a tribunal of twelve Olympians on a hill in Athens, later named for him, the Areiópagos (from *Areios págos*, the hill of Aris). The station of tribunals and juries was so strong in ancient Greece that even gods were brought before litigious prosecutors. Many later figures bear the name Areopagite, including Dionysios the Areopagite, whom Paul (Shaul) in Acts 17:34 converted on this hill named for the war god.

In the *Iliad*, Aris was fighting on the Trojan side. When Hera spotted him, she persuaded Zeus to have him wounded with a spear, after which he retreated to Mount Olympos. The worship of Aris as a god of war was not significant in Greece, but in

Rome, as mighty Mars, the cult of the god of power and empire was widespread. 111.

ARTEMIS. Twin sister of Apollo, the virgin moon goddess of forest and hunt, of healing and childbirth. Artemis's own birth is a foremost legend. When Hera discovered that her consort Zeus had made Lito (Leto) pregnant, she forbade Lito to bear her children (who would be Artemis and Apollo) on the mainland. The islands were also fearful of accepting the tainted Lito, but the floating island of Delos, treasure-house of Athens, agreed to receive her. Then Zeus secured the island to the sea bottom with four great pillars or, in another version, by means of alabaster chains. The islands floating around Delos, the Cyclades, were called white swans. They were held up by floating turtles. As Artemis's island, Delos was a holy island, on which no one could be born or die.

When the hunter Aktaion (Actaeon) discovered Artemis naked and saw her ravishing beauty, she turned him into a wild stag, which his own hounds tore apart and ate. As for the story of the virgin goddess's love affair with Aris, it is suspect. There were other men whom she was involved with, particularly Orion and Adonis, each of whom met his doom. Artemis's attribute beasts were the bear and the goat. Her central concern was virginity and the nymphs whom she trained to follow her, yet her representation in sculpture was often intensely sexual. The famous extant temple in Efesos contains a uniquely striking marble sculpture, whose torso is covered by erotic bumps that have been seen as large female nipples or bull testicles.

Artemis was also associated with the moon goddess Selini (Selene), who in later legend largely replaced her. In Rome Artemis was worshiped as Diana. 44a.

ATREIDAI (Atreidae). The Atreidai, usually referring to Agamemnon and Menelaos (Menelaus), are the descendants of Atreus. 27 incert.

ATREUS. Atreus was a king of Mykinai and father of Agamemnon and Menelaos. When his brother Thyestis tricked him into losing his throne, which he could only regain by reversing the track of the sun, he sought the aid of Zeus. Zeus made the sun move backward, and Atreus regained his throne. *See also* Atreidai.

ATTHIS. One of Sappho's friends, treated with deep affection in many poems. Like Anaktoria (q.v.), she leaves Sappho. 49, 96, 131.

DIKA. Probably short for Mnasidika (q.v.), one of Sappho's friends. 81.

DIONYSOS (Dionysius). Also called Bakhos (Bacchus, by the Romans), and Zagreus, the god of Orphism. A god of vegetation, wine, and spiritual ecstasy, he was worshiped with orgiastic rites and often represents the counterpart of Apollonian moderation. Dionysos was also a civilizing figure, a lawgiver, peacemaker, and protector of the theater and the other arts. But his lasting fame was as god of divine imagination and of wild and frenzied creativity.

In the Olympian tradition, Dionysos was the son of Zeus and Persefoni. He was also said to be the child of Zeus and Semili (Semele). The strange tale of his birth inspired mystery religions centering on this Orphic figure, as well as later plays, operas, and paintings. Zeus impregnated Semili, a mortal. Jealous Hera was furious when she discovered from Semili her affair with Zeus. Hera caused Semili's death, but Zeus rescued the fetal Dionysos by sewing him into his thigh, and a few months later, Dionysos was born.

After his birth, Dionysos was brought up by rain nymphs on Mount Nysa. The gifted boy soon invented the art of wine making. Hera, however, could not forgive his being sired by Zeus and struck him with madness, whereupon he became a wanderer in many lands. In Phrygia, Rhea cured him and taught him religious rites. Then he spent years in India, refining his philosophical resources, and bringing his secrets of wine making to many places in Asia. When he returned, satyrs, maenads, and nymphs followed him, and festivals of dance, song, wine, and ecstatic transcendence were celebrated to honor him. But his very knowledge of wine, the esoteric, and mystery rites frightened the more temperate, who dreaded the possibility of madness that art and ecstasy might bring with it.

Perhaps no Greek god other than Apollo has had so constant and profound an influence on all fields as the Dionysian deity. In Nietzsche's *Birth of Tragedy*, the philosopher compares the two tendencies in the Greek drama, the Dionysian, that of the ecstatic creator, with its peaks and pits, and the Apollonian, whose even virtues bring equanimity and refined insight. These attributes may apply to the baroque and romantic versus the archaic and classical, be it art, philosophy, or letters. There have been mystics, saints, and magicians who bore Dionysos's name. Apollo may have been Sappho's meter, but Dionysos was her love friend of dance mysteries and song, of beauty's summits and desolation's chasms. 17.

Dioskouroi (Dioscuri). Kastor (Castor) and Polydeukis (Pollux), the sons of Tyndareus, were twin hero warriors in Sparta after whom the constellation Dioscuri (Castor and Pollux) was named; they are its brightest stars. Kastor was a horseman, Polydeukis a boxer. Though they were "twins" through their mother, they had different fathers, Kastor being the son of Lida (Leda) and Tyndareus, and Polydeukis the son of Lida and Zeus, though often they are both identified as sons or descendents of king Tyndareus of Sparta. Their sisters were Helen and Klytemnestra. After Kastor died, he entreated Zeus to let Polydeukis share with him his own immortality, and Zeus arranged for them to divide their time between the night sky and dark Hades. He created a constellation for them alone called Gemini (Latin for "twins"), and they remain the patron stars of sailors. 166.

Doriha (Doricha). Probably a girlfriend of Sappho's brother Haraxos. 7; 15a, b.

Eros. God of love, child or attendant of Afroditi. Sappho makes Eros the son of Gaia (Ge, Earth) and Ouranos (Sky), but she most often uses *eros* to mean simply love that yearns for beauty, and especially for sexual union.

Sappho describes Eros as sweetbitter and cruel to victims.

Eros is not really the boy god but his metaphorical attribute: eros as difficult or joyous love and its erotic flame. Sappho, however, did not make this distinction in capital and lowercase letters, since ancient scrolls ran unpunctuated words together in capital letters. For her, Eros was already eros. While she prayed to and spoke with her ally Afroditi, she largely ignored the mischievous winged god who was to turn into Roman Cupid and, for later painters with Christian themes, a circling chubby cherub. 38, 44a, 54, 130.

GELLO. A ghost of a girl who died young and haunted little children in Lesbos. Apparently it is a term for children who die young, for unknown reasons, and haunt other children. *See* Zenobios *Proverbs* in "Sources, Notes, and Commentary." 178.

GERAISTION. A temple of Poseidon in Euboia. 96 (lines 21–37).

GONGYLA. One of Sappho's intimate friends. 22, 95.

GORGO. A rival of Sappho's; perhaps also a poet. 144.

GRACES (Harites). The three Graces were daughters of Zeus and Eurynomi, but are also said to have been daughters of Dionysos and Afroditi. Their names were Algaia, Eufrosyni, and Thalia. They were the personifications of grace and beauty. They were friends of the Muses, with whom they lived on Olympos. Their favored art was poetry—hence they were the poet's muse. 53, 103, 128.

GYRINNO, GYRINNA. One of Sappho's companions. In the poetic fragments she is Gyrinno, but she is Gyrinna in Maximus of Tyre's *Dissertations* 24.18.9, a commentary on homosexual love, which he compares to the Socratic art of love. 82a.

HADES. Hades refers both to the god and to his underground hell, a gloomy and unseen abyss of the dead ruled by Hades himself and Persefoni (Persephone). Hades was separated from the upper earth by the rivers Styx (hate), Lethe (oblivion), Aheron (sorrow), Flegethon (fire), and Kokytos (wailing). Hades was also said to be located in the far west beyond human habitation, possibly the vast unknown extending through the Atlantic Ocean. The god Hades is Pluto in Latin.

In the war with Hades' Titan father, Kronos, the Titanomachy (war of the titans), three of his sons, Zeus, Poseidon, and Hades, won. They confined Kronos to dark Tartaros (an earthly hell); Zeus took possession of the sky, Poseidon the sea, and Hades the underworld. Hades was visited by the famous, among whom were Orfeus, Theseus, Achilles, Odysseus, and Aeneas. By trickery he abducted Persefoni and made her his wife for six months a year. 55.

HARAXOS (Charaxos). Sappho's brother. 3, 5.

HEKTOR (HECTOR). Son of Priamos (Priam), husband of Andromache, and hero of the defense of Troy. Hektor was fated to die after he had killed Patroklas, Achilles' closest friend and lover. Raging with anger and vengeance, Achilles dragged Hektor's corpse three times around the walls of Troy to humiliate the hero's name. Hektor's funeral, portraying the grieving Andromache, is the last moving scene in the *Iliad*. 44.

HELEN (Eléna). Daughter of Zeus and Lida (Leda), of extraordinary beauty. As the wife of Menelaos, she was seduced and abducted by Paris to Troy and so became the overt cause of the Trojan War. But Helen as a personage and symbol of beauty and candid passion was much greater than the capsule tale of Paris's girlfriend who irresponsibly skipped off to Ilios (Ilium) and caused a ten-year war. The strongest of the counters to the story about Helen's venture to Troy is found in a poem by the great Sicilian poet Stisihoros (Stesichorus), who cynically states about the whole "white-horsed myth" in his mocking poem "Recantation to Helen: "I spoke nonsense and I begin again: / The story is not true. / You never sailed on a benched ship. / You never entered the city of Troy."* Plato, in the *Phaidros*, picks up on "the false accusation of Helen," giving the background of Stisihoros's

* Willis Barnstone, trans., *Sappho and the Greek Lyric Poets* (New York: Schocken Books, 1987, p. 110).

recantation: "When Stisihoros was blinded for having slandered Helen, he, unlike Homer, who was blinded for the same sin, wrote a palinode, a recantation, and immediately recovered his sight."

Of the many approaches, Sappho's is the most striking and convincing. She goes along with the Homeric legend but draws a different moral, making the power of love supreme. Yes, Helen left her worthy, dull, appointed husband, Menelaos, for the young Paris, but in her poem about her missing lover Anaktoria (16), who has also gone off to Sardis in the East, she cites Helen's escape to prove the ultimate worth of love, to which all may be sacrificed, including patriarchal conventions, family, and name. 16, 23.

HERA. Queen of the Olympian gods, daughter of Kronos and Rhea, and mother of Hefaistos and Aris. In Rome she was Juno. Hera was the patron goddess of marriage and childbirth, and, beginning at Minoan Kriti, she was worshiped in all ancient periods throughout Greece, and many temples were built to adore her. Her husband and brother was Zeus.

Despite Hera's notoriety for being a plague to the cheating Zeus, Hera was also a protector of women and a powerful divinity. Sappho saw her in this latter light. Hera appears as a goddess to whom one makes a pilgrimage. There is no hint of the abused and vengeful deity. Rather, she is the closest equivalent to Sappho's ally Afroditi; Sappho describes her as beautiful and dazzling, and she prays to her for help. *See* Artemis, *and also* Ares, Dionysos, *and* Zeus. 9, 17.

HERMIONI (Hermione). The only daughter of Menelaos and Helen. Her beauty did not match the beauty of her mother, Helen. When Helen eloped with Paris, Hermioni was left to be brought up by Agamemnon's wife, Klytemnestra. 23.

HERMIS (Hermes). Athletic son of Zeus and Maia, he was the cup-bearer and messenger of the gods and a psychopomp, that is, a guide of the dead to Hades. He was also the god of commerce, travelers, good luck, poets, and thieves and an extraordinary inventor credited with having invented music, the shepherd's lyre (made of cow intestines and tortoise shell), the flute, numbers, the alphabet, and gymnastics. As a messenger, he was represented with a winged hat, winged sandals, and a caduceus, a winged staff with two snakes twined around it that has become the emblematic staff of the medical profession. He was also a god of fertility and sexuality. His monument was usually the *herma*, a stone pillar with a head on top and a phallus in the center that was found outside houses as a good-luck symbol. Religious figures were named for him, most notably Hermis Trismegistos (thrice-strong Hermis), and there was the hermetic tradition in philosophy and magic. In literary criticism, we have hermeneutics, which is a method and theory of textual interpretation. Hermis was also a fun god, a humorous messenger often into mischief. He had three sons, of whom the best known was the satyr Pan, an amusing god of the woods and flocks, with a human torso and goat's legs and horns, whom Picasso resurrected with sensuality and glee. With Afroditi, Hermis fathered Hermafroditos, who became a hermaphrodite. In Rome Hermis was the popular Mercury. 141a, b.

HESPEROS. The evening star, son of Astraios or Kephalos or Atlas and Eos (Dawn), and father of the Hesperides. Hesperos is also the planet Venus (Afroditi). 104a, 104b.

HYMEN (Hymenaios). God of marriage, a handsome youth whom it was customary to invoke at Greek weddings by singing "Hymen, O Hymen," in the hymneal or bridal song. 111.

IDAOS. The herald or messenger, who is probably from Ida, a mountain area near Troy. In the *Iliad*, he appears as the chief herald of Troy. 44.

ILION (Ilium, Ilum) is the city of Troy (Troía), now called Hissarlik in Turkish. Homer's *Iliad* deals with the siege of Troy. It is not known whether the present site, the nine walls identified and excavated by Heinrich Schliemann in 1871, is actually Troy, where and whether the Trojan war actually took place, or whether Homer made a supreme amalgam of Bronze Age stories. There is no defining archeological or textual evidence of the events of the war. Near the Schliemann site is a Phrygian city called Troy, in a region known as the Troas or the Troad. 44.

ILOS. Father of Priamos (Priam) and founder of Troy. 44.

IONIAN. Referring to Greeks in an area of the west coast of Asia Minor. 98a.

IRANA (Oirana). One of Sappho's friends. Irana can be a friend's name or mean "peace." Its usage here is ambiguous. 91, 135.

JASON. Leader of the Argonauts, who set sail in the *Argo* to find the Golden Fleece, which he hoped to bring to his uncle Pelias in exchange for his patrimony. He obtained the fleece with the help of Medea, whom he later married. 152.

KASTOR (Castor). One of the Dioskouroi. See Dioskouroi. 166.

KLEANAKTIDAI. The children of Kleanax, including his son Myrsilos; they were a ruling family during Sappho's life. 98b.

KLEIS. Name of Sappho's daughter, also her mother, and perhaps a friend. 98b, 132.

KNOSSOS. Ancient capital of the Minoan kingdom and site of the palace of Minos, which has been associated with the labyrinth and the Minotaur (the bull of Minos). 2.

KOIOS (Coeus). A Titan, mother of Lito and hence grandmother of Apollo and Artemis. 44a.

KRITI. The island of Crete. 2.

KYDRO. A friend of Sappho's. 19.

KYPRIS (Cyprus). One of the names of Afroditi, meaning she is a Kyprian (Cypriote).

KYPROS. The large Greek island of Kypros (Cyprus), near the coast of Syria, was one of the chief seats of worship of Afroditi.

KYPROS-BORN (Cyprus-born). Another name for Afroditi. *See also* Afroditi.

KYTHEREIA (Kytherea, Cytherea). A surname of Afroditi, meaning one who comes from Kythera. Kythera was a city in Kriti (Crete). Kythera was also the name of one of the seven Ionian islands off the eastern coast of the Peloponnisos. Both the Kritan city of Kythera and the Ionian island of Kythera are associated with a seat for worshiping Afroditi. There was also a tradition that Afroditi rose from the sea near Kythera. *See also* Afroditi. 86, 140.

LESBIAN. *See* Lesbos.

LESBOS. The ancient name of the island of Mytilini, whose modern name comes from that of its main city in antiquity. The dialect of Lesbos was Aiolic, in which Sappho and Alkaios wrote. The name Lesbos is still used in speech, and also on maps, though usually in parenthesis. Lowercase "lesbian" refers to a woman whose sexual orientation is to women. 106.

LIDA (Leda). Mother of Helen, the Dioskouroi, and in some versions Klytemnestra, and wife of Tyndareus. She was seduced by Zeus, who came to her, as readers of Yeats know, in the form of a swan. Another version, to which Sappho alludes, has Nemesis lay an egg, which Lida found and cared for and from which came Helen. 166.

MEGARA. A friend of Sappho. 68a.

MIKA. Probably a shortened form of Mnasidika. Mika was a companion or a rival who had gone over to the house of Penthilos, a clan who were the ruling nobles of Mytilini. Sappho's family opposed the Penthelids, who had probably forced Sappho and her family to go into exile. 71.

MYTILINI (Mitylene). Ancient and modern capital of Lesbos, or Mytilini, where Sappho spent much of her life. The dialect of Lesbos was Aiolic, in which Sappho and Alkaios wrote.

MNASIDIKA. A friend of Sappho's who appears to have deserted her. *See also* Mika. 82a.

MUSES (Mousai). Daughters of Zeus and Mnemosyni (Memory), the nine muses lived on Mount Helikon, where they presided over the arts and sciences. They were worshiped early on in mountainous Pieria in Thessaly. Therefore, they were often called the Pierides. The muses were also worshipped on Mount Parnassos, and at Delfi, where Apollo was said to be their leader. 58, 103, 127, 128, 150.

MYRSILOS. Tyrant of Mytilini who probably caused the exile of Alkaios and Sappho.

NEREIDS. Sea nymphs, fifty daughters of Nereus. 5.

NEREUS. Son of Pontos, husband of the Oceanid Doris, and father of the Nereids, Nereus was the wise "old man of the sea." The Nereids often accompanied Poseidon and helped sailors in time of storm in the Mediterranean.

NIOBI (Niobe). Daughter of Tantalos and wife of Amfion, Niobi boasted to Lito that her family was larger than Lito's, and to avenge this insult Lito's children, Apollo and Artemis, killed the twelve to twenty children of Niobi. 142.

OLYMPOS (Olympus). Home of the Greek gods and the highest mountain in Greece. The Olympic Games were held every four years on the plains below the mountain in honor of Zeus. They included not only athletic events but contests of choral poetry and dance, and at times drama, which included choral dance. An Olympian was a Greek god or goddess. 27.

PAEAN. Epithet of Apollo. 44.

PAFIAN. Of Pafos (Paphos), and therefore Afroditi. *See also* Afroditi.

PANDION. King of Athens whose daughters Filomela and Prokni were turned into a swallow and a nightingale, respectively. (Latin tradition reversed the order.) The presence of a swallow often portended a forthcoming event. 135.

Peitho. The personification of persuasion, and the daughter or attendant of Afroditi. 96 (lines 21–37).

Penthilos. A rival family of ruling nobles in Mytilini. *See also* Mika, Mnasidika. 71.

Persefoni (Persephone). Daughter of Dimitir and Zeus, she was a goddess of fertility and vegetation and the unwilling queen of the underworld. In Sicily she was abducted by Hades and taken to the underworld, where he held her captive in his darknesses. Persefoni spent the winter in Hades and rose to the earth in the spring. She had a slight graveyard smell when she arrived, it was said, but she soon became flowery. Her return to the underworld signified the withering of flowers and grain.

The Eleusinian mysteries celebrated Persefoni's cycle of birth, death, and rebirth, in which she appeared under the name of Kore (a virgin). In Rome Persefoni was Proserpina or Proserpine. *See also* Afroditi, Dionysos. 158 Diehl.

Persuasion. *See* Peitho.

Phoebus (Foibus). An epithet of Apollo, meaning "shining." 44a.

Phokaia. A city of Ionia in Asia Minor, southeast of Mytilini. 101.

Pierian. Of Pieria, a region of Thrace in Macedonia, where the Muses were first worshiped. 103.

Pittakos. Tyrant, statesman, and sage of Lesbos in Sappho's time, depending on the view of the inhabitant; married the sister of Drakon; former ruler who was the son of Penthilos. Pittakos was initially an ally of both Alkaios's and Sappho's families, but later he joined with the party of another ruler, Myrsilos, an enemy of both Sappho and Alkaios. *See also* Myrsilos.

Pleiades. Seven daughters of Atlas and virgin companions of Artemis. When pursued by the giant hunter Orion, their prayers were answered when they were changed into doves (*pleiades*) and placed among the stars. Their names were Maia, Meropi, Elektra, Kelaino, Taygeti, Sterop (or Asteropi), and Alkyoni. 168b.

Polyanax. Father of Polyanaktidis and member of the important Polyanaktid family in Lesbos. 155.

Polydeukis (Pollux). One of the Dioskouroi. *See* Dioskouroi. 166.

Priamos (Priam). King of Troy during the Trojan war, he was the father of twenty children by Hecuba, including Hektor, Paris, and Kassandra. When his son Hektor was killed, he went into the Greek (Achaean) camp and begged Achilles for the body so he could be properly buried. Achilles agreed to the request. *See also* Hektor. 44.

Psapfo (Sappho). Born about 612 b.c.e. in either Eressos or Mytilini on the island of Lesbos, Sappho wrote lyric poems in her own Aiolic dialect, in which she referred to herself as Psapfo. 1; 65; 94; 133a, b.

Sappho. See Psapfo.

Sardis. Ancient city of Asia Minor and capital of the kingdom of Lydia. 96, 98a.

Semili (Semele). *See* Thyoni *and* Dionysos.

Thebe, Thebes. Not the more famous cities in Boitia and Egypt but a holy city near Mount Ida in the Troad in which Andromache's father, Etion, was both king and high priest.

Thyoni (Thyone), also known as Semili (Semele). Thyoni was the daughter of Kadmos and Zeus, and the mother of Dionysos. 17.

Tithonos. Brother of Priamos and lover of Eos (Dawn), who left him each morning. Through the prayers of Eos, he became immortal, but he did not retain his youth and so became synonymous with a decrepit old man. 58.

Tros. The mythical founder of Troy.

Tyndareus. A king of Sparta and Lida's husband; he fathered Helen, Klytemnestra, and the Dioskouroi, though most legends see him as a cuckold, with Zeus being the actual father of Helen and also of Polydeukis (Pollux).

Zeus or Dias. Son of Kronos and Rhea, brother of Poseidon, Hades, Hestia, Dimitir, and Hera, who was also his wife, Zeus was the supreme Olympic god. He determined good and evil as judge, and he carried the thunderbolt as his weapon of choice, though he had many powers of life, death, and transformation at his disposal. He was the archetypal Greek deity. At the same time, he was almost helplessly or whimsically human, resorting to all manner of disguises and metamorphoses to deceive his sister-wife Hera and conceal romances with other goddesses and mortals. 1, 17, 53, 96, 102.

BIBLIOGRAPHY
Editions, Studies, and Translations

Abbott, Sidney, and Barbara Love. *Sappho Was a Right-On Woman: A Liberated View of Lesbianism.* 1972. Reprint, New York: Stein and Day, 1985.

Balmer, Josephine. *Sappho: Poems and Fragments.* New York: Meadowland Books, 1993.

Barnard, Mary, trans. *Sappho.* Berkeley: University of California Press, 1958.

Barnstone, Willis. *The Poetics of Ecstasy: From Sappho to Borges.* New York: Holmes and Meier, 1983.

―――. *The Poetics of Translation: History, Theory, Practice.* New Haven: Yale University Press, 1993.

―――, trans. *Sappho and the Greek Lyric Poets.* Introduction by William E. McCulloh. New York: Schocken Books, 1987.

―――. *Sappho: Lyrics in the Original Greek with Translations.* Preface by A. R. Burn. New York: New York University Press, 1965. First published 1965 by Doubleday Anchor Books.

―――. *Sappho, Poems: A New Version.* Los Angeles: Sun and Moon Press, 1998.

Beaumont, Edith de, trans. *Poèmes de Sappho.* Illustrations by Marie Laurencin. One copy in the Kinsey Institute, Indiana University, Bloomington.

Bergk, T. *Poetae Lyrici Graeci.* 3 vols. Leipzig: B. G. Teubner, 1882.

Boardman, John, and E. La Rocca. *Eros in Greece.* London: Phaidon, 1978.

Bonnard, Andre, ed. and trans. *Poésies de Sappho.* Illustrations by Rodin. Lausanne: Mermod, 1948.

Bowie, A. M. *The Poetic Dialect of Sappho and Alcaeus.* New York: Arno Press, 1981.

Bowra, Cecil Maurice. *Greek Lyric Poetry: From Alman to Simonides.* 2nd rev. ed. Oxford: Oxford University Press, 1961.

Bremmer, Jan., ed. *From Sappho to de Sade: Moments in the History of Sexuality.* London: Routledge, 1989.

Burn, A. R. *The Lyric Age of Greece.* London: Edward Arnold, 1978.

Burnett, Anne Pippin. *Three Archaic Poets: Archilochus, Alcaeus, Sappho.* Cambridge, Mass.: Harvard University Press, 1983.

Campbell, David A. *The Golden Lyre: The Themes of the Greek Lyric Poets.* London: Duckworth, 1983.

———, ed. *Greek Lyric Poetry: A Selection.* London: Macmillan, 1967.

———, ed. and trans. *Sappho and Alcaeus.* Vol. 1 of *Greek Lyric.* Loeb Classical Library. Cambridge, Mass.: Harvard University Press, 1988.

Carson, Anne. *Eros the Bittersweet.* Princeton, N.J.: Princeton University Press, 1986.

———, trans. *If Not, Winter: Fragments of Sappho.* New York: Vintage Books, 2002.

Chandler, Robert, ed. and trans. *Sappho.* Introduction by Richard Jenkyns. London: J. M. Dent, 1998.

Davenport, Guy, trans. *Archilochos, Sappho, Alkman: Three Lyric Poets of the Late Greek Bronze Age.* Berkeley: University of California Press, 1980.

———, trans. *Poems and Fragments.* Ann Arbor: University of Michigan Press, 1965.

———, trans. *Seven Greeks.* New York: New Directions, 1995.

Davison, J. A. *From Archilochus to Pindar.* London: Macmillan, 1968.

Diehl, Ernest. *Anthologia Lyrica Graeca.* Vol. 1. Leipzig: B. G. Teubner, 1964.

Dover, K. J. *Greek Homosexuality.* London: Duckworth, 1978.

Duban, Jeffrey M. *Ancient and Modern Images of Sappho: Translations and Studies in Archaic Greek Love Lyric.* Lanham, Md.: University Press of America, 1983.

DuBois, Page. *Sappho Is Burning.* Chicago: University of Chicago Press, 1995.

Edmonds, J. M., ed. and trans. *Lyra Graeca.* Vol. 1. 2nd printing. London: William Heinemann, 1928.

Fränkel, Hermann. *Early Greek Poetry and Philosophy.* Translated by

Moses Hadas and James Willis. New York: Harcourt Brace Jovanovich, 1962.

Freedman, Nancy Mars. *Sappho: The Tenth Muse*. New York: St. Martin's Press, 1998.

Gentili, Bruno. *Poetry and Its Public in Ancient Greece*. Translated by A. Thomas Cole. Baltimore: Johns Hopkins University Press, 1988.

Gerber, D. E. *Euterpe: An Anthology of Early Greek Lyric, Elegiac and Iambic Poetry*. Amsterdam: Hakkert, 1970.

Grahn, Judy. *The Highest Apple: Sappho and the Lesbian Poetic Tradition*. San Francisco: Spinsters Ink, 1985.

Greek Anthology. Edited by W. R. Paton. 5 vols. Cambridge, Mass.: Harvard University Press, 1916–1918.

Green, Ellen, Ellen, ed. *Reading Sappho: Reception and Transmission*. Berkeley: University of California Press, 1996.

———, ed. *Re-Reading Sappho: Reception and Transmission*. Berkeley: University of California Press, 1996.

H.D. (Hilda Doolittle). *Notes on Thought and Vision, and The Wise Sappho*. London: Peter Owen, 1988.

Hutchinson, G. O. *Greek Lyric Poetry: A Commentary on Selected Larger Pieces: Alcman, Stesichorus, Sappho, Alceaus, Ibycus, Anacreon, Simonides, Bacchylides, Pindar, Sophocles, Euripides*. Oxford: Oxford University Press, 2001.

Jay, Peter and Caroline Lewis, eds. *Sappho through English Poetry*. London: Anvil Press Poetry, 1996.

Jenkyns, R. *Three Classical Poets: Sappho, Catullus, Juvenal*. Cambridge, Mass.: Harvard University Press, 1982.

Kirkwood, Gordon M. *Early Greek Monody*. Cornell Studies in Classical Philology 37. Ithaca, N.Y.: Cornell University Press, 1974.

Lattimore, Richmond, trans. "Sappho: Selections." In *Greek Lyrics*. 2nd ed. Chicago: University of Chicago Press, 1960.

Ledwidge, Bernard. *Sappho: La première voix d'une femme*. Paris: Mercure de France, 1987.

Lefkowitz, Mary R. *Heroines and Hysterics*. London: Duckworth, 1981.

Lobel, Edgar, and Denys Page, eds. *Poetarum Lesbiorum Fragmenta*. Oxford: Oxford University Press, 1955.

Lombardo, Stanley. *Poems and Fragments*. Edited by Susan Warden; introduction by Pamela Gordon. Indianapolis: Hackett, 2002.

Longinus. *Longinus on Sublimity.* Translated by D. A. Russell. Oxford: Oxford University Press, 1966.

———. *On the Sublime.* Edited by D. A. Russell. Oxford: Oxford University Press, 1964.

Marx, Olga, and Ernst Morwitz, trans. *Poems of Alcman, Sappho, Ibycus.* New York: Alfred A. Knopf, 1945.

Nims, John Frederick. *Sappho to Valéry: Poems in Translation.* New Brunswick, N.J.: Rutgers University Press, 1971.

Page, Denys. *Epigrammata Graeca.* Oxford: Oxford University Press, 1975.

———. *Poetae Melici Graeci.* Oxford: Oxford University Press, 1962.

———. *Sappho and Alcaeus: An Introduction to the Study of Ancient Lesbian Poetry.* Oxford: Clarendon Press, 1979.

———. *Sappho and Alcaeus.* Oxford: Oxford University Press, 1959.

Picasso, Pablo. *Grâce et mouvement: 14 compositions originales, gravées sur cuivre.* Edited by Louis Grosclaude. Issued in portfolio. "Sappho, 14 poèmes," pp. 17–32. Zurich: Presses des Conzett and Huber, 1943.

Pomeroy, Sarah. *Goddesses, Whores, Wives, and Slaves: Women in Classical Antiquity.* New York: Schocken Books, 1975.

Pope, Alexander. *The Works of Alexander Pope Esq.* Vol. 3, *Consisting of Fables, Translations, and Imitations.* London: printed for H. Lintot, 1736.

Powell, Jim, trans. *Sappho, a Garland: The Poems and Fragments.* New York: Farrar, Straus, Giroux, 1993.

Prins, Yopie. *Victorian Sappho.* Princeton, N.J.: Princeton University Press, 1999.

Quasimodo, Salvatore. *Lirici greci.* Translated by Luciano Anceschi. Milan: A. Mondadori, 1960.

Rabinowitz, Nancy Sorkin. *Among Women: From the Homosocial to the Homoerotic in the Ancient World.* Austin: University of Texas Press, 2002.

Rayor, Diane J., trans. *Sappho Poems.* With illustrations by Janet Steinmetz. Colorado Springs: Press at Colorado College, 1980.

Reynolds, Margaret. *History of Sappho.* New York: Vintage Books, 1999.

———. *The Sappho History.* New York: Palgrave Macmillan, 2003.

Rissman, Leah. *Love as War: Homeric Allusion in the Poetry of Sappho.* Konigstein, Germany: Hain, 1983.

Robinson, David Moore. *Sappho and Her Influence*. New York: Cooper Square Publishers, 1963.

Roche, Paul, trans. *The Love Songs of Sappho*. Introduction by Page Dubois. New York: Signet Classic, 1991.

Rosenmeyer, Thomas G., James W. Halporn, and Martin Ostwald. *The Meters of Greek and Latin Poetry*. New York: Bobbs-Merrill, 1963.

Segal, Charles. *Aglaia: The Poetry of Alcman, Sappho, Pindar, Bacchylides, and Corinna*. Lanham, Md.: Rowman & Littlefield, 1998.

Snyder, Jane McIntosh. *Lesbian Desire in the Lyrics of Sappho*. New York: Columbia University Press, 1997.

Treu, Max, ed. and trans. *Sappho*. Munich: Ernst Heimeran Verlag, 1963.

Voigt, Eva-Maria, ed. *Sappho et Alcaeus: Fragmenta*. Amsterdam: Athenaeum, 1971.

West, M. L. *Greek Metre*. New York: Oxford University Press, 1982.

Wilamowitz-Moellendorff, Ulrich von. *Sappho und Simonides*. Berlin: Weidmann, 1966.

Wilhelm, James J. *Gay and Lesbian Poetry: An Anthology from Sappho to Michelangelo*. New York: Garland, 1995.

Wilson, Lyn Hatherly. *Sappho's Sweetbitter Songs: Configurations of Female and Male in Ancient Greek Lyric*. New York: Routledge, 1996.

INDEX OF POEMS AND FRAGMENTS BY NUMBER

Note: The poem and fragment numbers in this index reflect the numbering system used in this edition. For more information on the ordering of the texts with respect to other editions, see the Introduction, pages xli–xliii.